1/7/2016
Donna an
May Gods love,
be ever present in your lives. Thank
you for sharing your testimony.

MIRACLES
Still HAPPEN

WE ARE WITNESSES
TO GOD'S KINGDOM WORKS

Gloria Penn

GLORIA PENN

xulon
PRESS

Copyright © 2015 by Gloria Penn

Miracles Still Happen
We Are Witnesses to God's Kingdom Works
by Gloria Penn

Printed in the United States of America

ISBN 9781498455169

All rights reserved solely by the author. The author guarantees all contents are original and do not infringe upon the legal rights of any other person or work. No part of this book may be reproduced in any form without the permission of the author. The views expressed in this book are not necessarily those of the publisher.

Unless otherwise indicated, scripture quotations are taken from The Good News for Modern Man (GNMM). Copyright © 1996 by Zondervan; The New Revised Standard Version (NRSV). Copyright © 1989 by National Council of Churches of Christ; The New Revised Standard Version (NRSV). Copyright © 1997 by World Bible Publishers, Inc.; The New International Version (NIV). Copyright © 2002 by Zondervan; The Today's Parallel Bible—King James Version. Copyright © 2000 by Zondervan; The New American Bible (NAB). Copyright © 1970 by Confraternity of Christian Doctrine; New American Standard Bible (NASB) Copyright © 1995 by The Lockman Foundation; New King James Version (NKJV) Copyright: © 1982 by Thomas Nelson Bibles. Used by permission. All rights reserved

www.xulonpress.com

Content

Foreword ix
Acknowledgements xi
Preface xiii

I. THE ASSURANCE OF THINGS HOPED FOR 17
Chapter 1   A Journey of Faith 19
               Buying a Home in Tulsa 28
               The Miracle of Receiving the Holy Spirit
                 and the Call 33
Chapter 2   Christ, the Giver of Salvation and
              the King of Miracles 41
               Miracle in Classroom 211 45
Chapter 3   Miracles of Healing 52
               George Frey—Healed of Pleurisy 52
               The Healing of George's Friend, John 57
               The Healing of Our Son, Mark 58
               The Healing of Our Son, Stephen 63
               God Cares about Little Things—Gloria 65
               The Miraculous Healing of Earl Chandler 67
               The Miraculous Healings of the
                 Silankas Family 68
               The Healing of My Back—Gloria 72
Chapter 4   Prayer and Miracles 74

Miracles Still Happen

Chapter 5	Testimonies: Miracles of Healing	79
	The Healing of Gloria Bovankovich	79
	Healing of Donna Rust	82
	Headaches —No Match for the Power of God (shared by Eleanor Allen)	83
	A Miracle (shared by Jeri Henry):	86
	Two Miracles (shared by Cheryl Thompson)	86
	A Miracle (shared by Sister Willie Mae Crump)	87
	A Knee Is Miraculously Healed (shared by Gayle Harold)	88
	A Miracle (shared by Annette Moore)	90
	Miracle of Buying a Home (shared by Joan Carter)	91
	The Healing of Evangelist Marinda Turner	92
	Gloria Moore (in her words)	96
	The Healing of Gwendolyn Jones	98
Chapter 6	God Works Miracles in Mysterious Ways	102
	Miracles of God's Intervention in Unexpected Ways	104
	God Gives Us Our Hearts' Desire (John's trip to the Inauguration)	106
	A Miracle of Persistent Faith	107
	A Miracle of Protection	112

II. THE EVIDENCE OF THINGS UNSEEN 115

Chapter 7	The Miracle of the Holy Spirit	117
Chapter 8	Going From East to West—A Miracle that Takes Its Own Time	126
Chapter 9	The Importance of Forgiving as It Relates to Miracles	132
	Unforgiveness/Forgiveness	135
	Forgiveness in Marriage	139

Chapter 10 The Miracle of God's Presence and Peace ...143
Chapter 11 Miracles Happen When We Listen to God ...150
Chapter 12 Fasting Into the Presence of God 155
     The Presence of Christ and His
      Healing Grace in Holy Communion 158
Chapter 13 The Holy Spirit Miraculously Guides Us 160
     The Importance of Professing the
      Word/Promises of God 163
     Miracles of God's Provisions 165
Chapter 14 A Day to Remember (When Miracles
     Don't Seem to Happen) 170
     Our Grandson Comes Home 175
     God Miraculously Uses What We Have 183
Chapter 15 Faith, Mover of Limitations, Catalyst
     of Miracles 186
     The Healing of Greg Harrison Through
      Prayers of Faith 190
     Stepping Out in Faith to Trust the Lord 195

APPENDIX
Sermon—Love and Compassion Without Limitations 201

Foreword

In this world that is filled with concerns and unbelief, people are looking for the hand of God and want to see Him working in their midst. They have experienced setbacks, illnesses, loss and problems of every kind. Some Christians will tell you they have looked for a miracle in the middle of difficult circumstances and could not see one.

There are many instances of miracles throughout the Bible. Jesus was constantly performing miracles for the people and miracles are happening this very day. Generally, people think miracles took place during the time of Christ, but they actually don't happen in our current society. But often they are overlooked because of our very busy lives, or we think that an unusual or miraculous healing was just luck or coincidence. And, of course, there is unbelief. Rev. Gloria Penn shows throughout this work just how a closer walk with the Lord is key to seeing and experiencing who He is.

When God intervenes into the affairs of man, miracles do happen. When we pray and seek God's face and believe that He has all power to do what He said He would do, miracles happen. When we don't give up after a few prayers and a few years of asking for God to move in our lives, miracles happen. God loves us and wants to show us He is still God and that He is sovereign.

Throughout this book, you will see examples of miracles taking place. There are numerous times you will see the hand of God moving—from the ordinary to the extraordinary. Rev. Penn has chronicled a number of occasions where miracles have taken place in the life of her family as well as in the lives of various friends. Without question, in every instance, it was truly an act of God.

Rev. Penn uses this book to take the reader through a wonderful and spiritual journey of dependence on and belief in the Almighty God. She so eloquently displays God's healing power and shows that this same power has been given to us by and through the Holy Spirit.

This is an excellent book that will help you to look for and believe in miracles. As I read through chapter after chapter, I found so much that enriched my life and encouraged me to always be still and "know that He is God." I have been able to grow spiritually even after being a Christian for 60 years.

This book has caused me to re-examine some of my thoughts and attitudes and has given me a powerful sensitivity to seeking and hearing from God.

> Willie Mae Reid Crump, Author
> and Spiritual/Inspirational Writer
> Roswell, Georgia

Author of *Rhymes for Reasons: A Personal Journey of Praise and Prayer*

Acknowledgment

It is with great appreciation that I acknowledge the support of my husband, Reverend Dr. John I. Penn. His commitment and faithfulness to God has been a great inspiration to me. He has constantly encouraged me to complete the writing of this book and consistently given me his love, prayers, and spiritual support. I would like to thank God for my children, John II, Myrtle, Jacqueline, Mark, Christina and Stephen, for whom the Lord answered countless number of prayers. My friends have also given me spiritual support and encouragement, particularly those in our intercessory prayer group, Virtuous Women, and those who trusted me enough to share their testimonies in this book. Without the guidance of the Holy Spirit and the strength and protection of God, in Christ, this book could not have been written. The Holy Spirit has truly made this book possible and has been an ever present guide throughout my years of writing it. As the Scripture reveals, the Holy Spirit is the Spirit of Truth and if we know the truth, the truth will set us free.

Preface

Miracles Still Happen has been influenced by the life I have been blessed to live. My spiritual journey began even before my birth, when my parents prayed and thanked God for me. At the age of three, my mother, Mrs. Genevieve Parker, taught me to pray, and she read and told me stories based on biblical accounts. She also taught me to play the piano. The strong commitment to church and love for God demonstrated by my father, Dr. H.L. Parker, also greatly influenced my life. I was so impressed by the biblical stories my mother read, that when I came across one of my parents' Bibles at the age of six, I began to read it for myself. I remember that I kept it under my bed and deeply cherished the things I read. I was particularly touched by the compassion and power of Jesus Christ.

This, along with the teachings I heard in Sunday school, inspired me to want to give my life to Christ. There are those who believe young children do not understand enough to commit their lives to Jesus, but even at that young age, from the powerful accounts of his love and works, I knew he was a most special person, and I wanted to know him better. So when I was six, while standing outside and thinking and reflecting about the Living God, I looked up towards the sky and asked Jesus to come into my heart and life. Immediately,

I knew the Lord answered my simple childlike request; from then on, there was a definite change in my life.

These two things my mother introduced me to, the Word of God and music, have influenced my life greatly throughout the years. At age seven I was invited to speak at a Vacation Bible School program. Experiencing what God could do through someone as quiet and ordinary as me, helped me realize that God had something special for me to do with my life.

This spiritual foundation continued to be an important part of my life as I grew older. I graduated from high school at the age of fifteen and went on to college to major in music. Three-and-a-half years later, I had completed my course work; the following May, I graduated magna cum laude. After teaching for a few months, I studied towards a master's degree in music education at Boston University. I completed most of my graduate work at Boston University before I married John; within a few years, we had three of our six children.

Although I was well aware of God's blessings, once I had a family, I faced many more challenges. I needed answers and encouragement. This is when I committed to reading the Bible on a regular basis. The Psalms and the Gospels gave me the hope I needed. But as I read more and more, I began to wonder why I did not see the miracles of the Gospel being revealed in my life and the lives of those around me. I was particularly amazed at the healing miracles performed by Jesus.

One day, while driving my children to school, I heard a preacher on the radio talk about the healing power of Jesus, confirming the things I had read. I was really excited with the new discovery that we could, even in this day and time, ask Jesus to heal us, and he continues to move in other miraculous ways in our lives. It was then that I started my quest for

Preface

a closer relationship with God and began to see the workings of God's grace in profound ways. This quest helped me to build a foundation of belief toward seeing the manifestation of the miraculous accounts related in this book.

After my husband, John I. Penn, responded to the call of God on his life, we witnessed—in our family, with our friends, and with strangers— many miracles of God's love and compassion in Jesus Christ. We were amazed that God would use ordinary people like us, through prayer, to help manifest miraculous works and do so in ways we sometimes least expected. As further testimony to the works of God through and in ordinary people, in the power of the Holy Spirit, accounts of miracles in the lives of others are also included in this book, giving added evidence that God's love and power are available to all who ask. It was while we were still lay persons in the church that God blessed us to begin seeing and experiencing many miracles through our personal prayers. John and I are now both ordained ministers, and we continue to see demonstrated in our ministry the love and compassion of Jesus Christ.

This book is written to give hope, encouragement, and evidence to all who may read it, that in the lives of those who love and trust the Lord, God does intervene. God does so in ways we never imagine or think possible. Just as we read in the Gospels how Jesus demonstrated the love and compassion of God, God continues to do this through the Holy Spirit. As Scripture so clearly reminds us, God is indeed the same, yesterday, today, and forever.

Gloria J. Parker Penn

I. THE ASSURANCE OF THINGS HOPED FOR

In this age of many amazing scientific and medical discoveries, as well as the wonderful developments of technology, we have come to realize that much can be accomplished through humankind's intelligence and hard work. We see the fruits of it everywhere as we live our daily lives, in our businesses, in our homes, in technology, in medicine, and in the future of the space age. Yes, humankind can achieve much beyond the ordinary.

In spite of all of these accomplishments, things are happening that far surpass human intelligence and knowledge. There are extraordinary happenings from the hand of God that no matter how humankind attempts to explain them, in human terms they are still beyond human understanding. These things are often called miracles. Yes, even in the midst of disasters, trials and tribulations, as well as disappointments, miracles still happen. God reaches down from God's throne of grace and reveals an everlasting and outreaching love. Still, many doubt that miracles, particularly in our time, can happen or still happen. In the following pages, we will hopefully come to understand and agree that miracles have happened, miracles are still happening, and miracles will continue to happen!

One

A Journey of Faith

In the summer of 1974, my husband, John, began to feel very strongly that God was leading him to go to graduate school to study and prepare himself for the ordained ministry. After some prayer and discussion, we felt that perhaps Oral Roberts University was the best school for our situation. We realized that going to ORU would be a challenge, to say the least, but it seemed that God was urging us on to do the impossible—to trust and totally depend on Him.

Our walk of faith began with John resigning his job in response to God's call on his life. This was not a decision we could take lightly; we had six children and the income John received was very much needed. In addition, if John decided to go to school in Tulsa, Oklahoma, we would have to sell our home and move, taking our six children—John, Myrtle, Jacqueline, Mark, Christina and Stephen (the last two being, sixteen months and four months old, respectively)—with us. How many wives, having six children, would agree to their husbands resigning their job and feel they are in their right mind? Wanting to be as sure as we could that God was leading us, John and I prayed diligently. In response to our prayers, we were affirmed that God would take care of us.

God also revealed that he wanted John to go to school and the school God had chosen was Oral Roberts University.

In obedience to what we felt God was telling us to do, John completed an application to be accepted as a student in the School of Theology of Oral Roberts University. We had heard Dr. Howard Ervin, a professor of ORU, speak at a Full Gospel Meeting in Pennsylvania. That evening, Dr. Ervin stated that he had a strong feeling someone there would soon be a student at ORU. We didn't think it was John, but John did decide to walk to the front and ask those at the meeting to pray that if it was God's will, he would be accepted as a student. Soon after, in August, John inquired of the registrar's office concerning his acceptance as a student. He was advised not to come, because a decision could not be made until all of the required transcripts were received from all of the schools John had attended. There were five schools in all, including John's high school; A.M. and N College now the University of Arkansas at Pine Bluff; Virginia State in Petersburg, Virginia; and the University of Delaware.

After more prayer, John decided that we should see for ourselves if ORU was the place to go. We did not want to presume that God was leading us in this direction. We planned to take the trip in faith, trusting the Lord to take care of us. John prayed for over $300.00 to take the trip, and we set the date for the last two weeks of August. Such a trip would require us to travel about 1250 miles over several days. In the meantime, we continued to pray for confirmation to go.

In preparation for the trip, our good friend and prayer partner, Anthony Santucci, serviced our station wagon and added an extra seat, making sure it was mechanically sound. To encourage us and help with our finances, he also gave us a financial love gift. We began to pack our bags with the expectancy that somehow we would be financially able to go. Before leaving, John again checked with the registrar's office by telephone to find out if he had been accepted. Again they told him that all of his records had not arrived from the other schools, and they advised him not to come until all of his records were in. John even consulted with a well-known evangelist who also advised us not to go without the necessary funds. To make things more discouraging, the date we had set to begin the journey arrived, and we only had $117.00.

In the normal and sensible way of thinking, it seemed that it was best for us not to take the trip, but after more prayer, we decided to go. We planned for our first stop to be in John's hometown, Roanoke, Virginia, about a six-hour drive from Delaware. Our plan was to stay overnight at his mother's home. While there, John's mother asked if we knew that when we prayed for his brother, Jimmy, two years earlier, he had been instantly healed by God. We had not known, and this was certainly exciting news to us. We wanted to hear what had happened directly from Jimmy, so we got into our car and rushed over to his home.

Two years earlier, during a short visit with Jimmy and his wife Jeanette, Jimmy informed us that he had a very painful ulcer that limited what he could eat. I urged John to pray for him. We placed our hands on Jimmy, and John prayed a simple prayer, asking God to heal his brother. We left without any idea that Jimmy had been instantly healed. Now, after arriving at Jimmy's home, John asked, "Why didn't you let us know that you were healed?" Jimmy simply said, "You are the one who came here talking about healing; I didn't know anything about healing. Since you are the one who knew about healing, I felt you also knew I was healed." Jimmy let us know that from the moment we ended our prayers for his healing, he had no more discomfort or pain and could eat anything he wanted to eat.

Supported by this good news that clearly reminded us of God's healing power and miracles, we continued on our way. A few hours before arriving in Knoxville, we stopped at the welcome travel center in Tennessee, and John called the registrar's office once more. When he came back, he related that the registrar's office continued to advise him not to come because all of his records were still not in. We prayed again. We had already traveled about five hundred miles, so after praying, we decided to continue on to Knoxville. We arrived in Knoxville late in the evening. Knowing that we needed a place to stay for the night, John went to a phone booth and made a call to a Catholic parish. He related to the priest that we were a Catholic charismatic family with six children and were looking for a place to spend the night and have fellowship. The priest told John that a Catholic charismatic family, the Eyrings, would be able to accommodate us.

Following the directions given to us by the priest, we arrived a few hours later at a large, lovely home in an exclusive neighborhood of Knoxville. We were welcomed by the Eyrings with open arms and were pleased to find out, as we were introduced, that they had five children. Our children joined their younger children while the two older girls graciously prepared dinner for us.

Meanwhile, we were invited to sit and talk with the Eyrings in their spacious living room. We shared with them concerning the purpose of our trip and why we were in Knoxville. Time seemed to pass quickly, and before we knew it, the girls had finished preparing dinner. Together, both families sat down to eat a delicious meal. We could truly see God's hand in providing so wonderfully for our family. After dinner, we continued our conversation. Dr. Eyring, an orthopedic surgeon, told us about some of the unusual operations he had performed. He then related that just that day, while performing an operation, he felt like the joints in his finger were going to break. As an orthopedic surgeon, it is very important that your fingers are in good working condition and pain free. In addition, he had been having a lot of back pain.

John and I immediately looked at each other. We were both thinking about the instructions of Christ in Luke 10: *"When you enter a house, first say, 'Peace to this house'"* (v. 5). This we had done when we first met the Eyrings at their door. Then the Scripture says, *"Stay in that house eating and drinking whatever they give you, for the worker deserves his wages. Do not move around from house to house'* (v. 7). Verse 9 states, *"Heal the sick who are* there, *and tell them 'The kingdom of God is near you."* We had been trusting in these words before we started the trip and so, we looked at each other with expectancy—with that special knowing in our hearts that God had us there for a purpose. John asked Ed did he believe in divine healing, and if so, could we pray for him. Ed answered, "Yes." That was all we needed to hear. We asked Mrs. Eyring to join us and just as Jesus gave his disciples the authority to do, we placed our hands on Ed. John prayed that God would heal him, both his fingers and his back, in the name of Jesus. Immediately afterwards, Ed commented that he had no more pain. We rejoiced that Ed was healed.

The next morning, after a very restful sleep, Mrs. Eyring prepared a delicious breakfast for us and sent us on our way. As we traveled, John and I noted how peaceful and quiet the children were. There were no fights or spats among them. It was as if the Lord had directed an envoy of angels to travel with us to make sure that everything progressed smoothly, and I'm sure God did!

After about eight hours of driving, now on our third day, we arrived in Little Rock, Arkansas. Parking outside of a restaurant, John, as he had done before, went to the pay phone to see if he could make a contact for a place to stay that night. While he was calling, I had the strangest feeling about where we were and sensed, even before John returned to the car, that we were not supposed to stay in Little Rock. When John returned, I knew what the answer would be; he was unable to contact anyone. As I continued to sense an eeriness about that place, I was reminded of how Paul, when trying to go into Bithynia (Acts 16.7) was not permitted by the Holy Spirit to do so. Without another thought, I said to John, "I feel that we should drive on." John looked at me and said, "Are you sure? I've been driving all day." Somehow, I was definitely sure, so we continued on. John, though tired, drove all that night, only stopping briefly at a rest stop for some sleep. When he awoke, we continued on until we reached Tulsa and Oral Roberts University.

We arrived at ORU about 5:00 a.m. Later, when we were awakened by a sound of students walking on campus, John decided to go to the prayer tower where he shared his concern with one of the ladies there. This "little old lady" as he calls her, prayed a powerful prayer with him. After leaving the Prayer Tower, to go to the Registrar's Office, the song, "Something Good is Going to Happen to You," the theme song of the ministry of ORU, kept going through his mind.

As John walked into the Registrar's Office, the lady there asked, "May I help you?" He told the lady in charge of the Registrar's Office that he was from Delaware and was there to find out if his transcripts were in. Surprisingly, the lady laughed and laughed. Finally she said, "Oh, you must be Mr. Penn! You came even though I told you not to come. All of your transcripts arrived right after I spoke to you yesterday." Here again was an example and proof of the old saying, "The Lord is always on time," or as a popular gospel song goes, "God is an on time God." What good news that was and an answer to prayer. The registrar continued, "I'm going to do something I never do. Take these records to the Theology Department to see Dr. Horner and Dr. Irving."

John immediately took the folder with his records to the office of Dr. Horner in the Theology department. He met with Dr. Horner and after some discussion, Dr. Horner looked over John's records and said that he saw no reason John should not be approved as a student in the Theology department. He did make it clear that John's admission would need to be approved by the committee, and he would need to complete eighteen course hours. This was because John's undergraduate degree was in music education, not in theology. We now realized why it was so important for John to continue driving from Little Rock, rather than stopping there. Because John continued on, driving through the night, we arrived on Thursday. If we had arrived on Friday, none of the professors would have been available to look over John's records or discuss with him the possibilities of attending ORU. On Fridays the professors and students attended chapel, after chapel, school was dismissed so that the professors and students could participate in evangelism.

Dr. Horner then asked John if he had a place to stay. John responded that he had no place to stay and that his family was with him. To our amazement and surprise, Dr. Horner invited us, with our six children, to stay with him and his wife.

Dr. Horner and his wife, Anne, had a beautiful home in Tulsa that had recently been damaged by a tornado. They and their two children were living in a comparatively small townhouse until their home was repaired. In spite of this, Dr. Horner and Anne welcomed us with open arms. Even though there was now a crowd, in their townhouse, everything went well. Anne prepared dinner for us and the children were peaceful.

After dinner, Dr. Horner invited John to go with him to a charismatic meeting where he had been invited as a guest speaker. Dr. Horner shared with the people concerning his trip to Russia where he met with many Christians. He shared that in Russia there were many people of strong faith, who meet in secret and memorize Scripture because they could not openly profess their faith. The government did not approve of Christians meeting together. Afterwards, Dr. Horner asked John to share his testimony. Dr. Horner and John then prayed for the needs of the people. As they prayed together, many people were healed and the Holy Spirit moved in a powerful way.

The next morning, Dr. Horner came to John and told him that he had been given a large amount of money by the group they shared with, and he wanted to give John a part of it. Again, God was meeting our needs. That evening, John and I were invited by the Horners to attend a prayer meeting in the home of one of their neighbors, the Wells. They asked us to share, and we shared on the importance of the family and how God had blessed our family and kept us together as husband and wife. We were then given the wisdom of the Holy Spirit to pray for the healing of family relationships. Several people came forth and asked for prayer concerning broken relationships, including a mother and daughter. God, through the Holy Spirit, beautifully blessed them to be healed in their relationships. It was truly a blessing to see God's love being manifested among those present.

The next morning, as I was thinking about how God had blessed us to travel over 1200 miles from Delaware to Oklahoma, I suddenly had the desire to go and see my mother. Because of the distance, I had not seen my parents for several years, and they had not seen my younger children who were still babies. Getting to Lorman, Mississippi, where they lived and were professors at Alcorn University, would take another day of driving. But, after seeing what God had done, I knew it was possible. I expressed my desire to go and visit with them to John and he replied, "We don't have enough money, but if God provides what we need, we will go." Almost as soon as we finished talking, one of the ladies who had attended the prayer meeting arrived at the Horner's home and asked to speak to John. She expressed to John how the Lord had blessed her to be able to save a great deal of money for God's work. She continued, "God has placed it on my heart to give you a love offering." This she did, and much to my joy and surprise, we had just enough money to visit my parents.

The next morning, after a good breakfast and an exchange of hugs with the Horners, we piled into the station wagon and headed for Lorman, to visit my parents, Dr. H. L. and Mrs. Genevieve Parker. After a long day's journey, we arrived on the campus of Alcorn State and finally at the home of my parents. They were greatly surprised to see us.

What a visit! We shared with them about our experiences in the Lord, and our trip, including God's many blessings. They had an opportunity to see their grandchildren, and our grandchildren to see and talk to their grandparents. I never dreamed that I would have the opportunity to see them during this trip, but God knew. God blesses us, at times, more than we can imagine. Before we left the next day, we prayed for our parents, and they sent us on our way with their blessings. God had performed another miracle!

Returning to Delaware was smooth sailing. We stopped to see Dr. Eyring at his office. He told us how he was healed, when we prayed together and asked if John would come in and pray for a nurse, who was his secretary. She was experiencing stomach problems and was in need of healing. After John prayed for Dr. Eyring's secretary, we continued on our way home. With the money we had left, we purchased more gas, stayed overnight in a hotel and had a delicious huge pizza. The next day, we headed back home to Newark,

Delaware. Before we arrived home, I reminded John that it would be good to get a few groceries, which he did. Once we were home, I did something that I never remember doing before. Because I was concerned that we would have enough money for the children to begin school, I asked John how much money he had in his wallet. I watched as John began to count the money and place it on the dresser in our bedroom. First he counted the dollar bills, then the large change, and then, to our amazement, as he counted down to the last penny, there was $117.00 exactly! This was the same amount that we began the trip with. What a miracle! We had traveled for nine days, purchased food for a family of eight as we traveled, and gas for a trip of over 2,900 miles. Yet, we had the same amount of money that we started with. The entire trip had been on the Lord. Furthermore, we never shared with anyone our financial needs. God showed us a miracle comprised of several other miracles, and we knew without a doubt that John was to attend Oral Roberts. We knew without a doubt that God would take care of us. We knew without a doubt that God intended for us to move to Tulsa.

Buying a Home in Tulsa

In December of 1974, John and I, with our six children, moved to Tulsa. We accepted the invitation of Professor Horner to stay in their home until we could find a suitable place for our family to live. We immediately began to look around, search the papers, and contact real estate agents; but we were still having a difficult time finding a place to purchase that was suitable for our family. Finally, we were introduced to a Christian real estate agent. He was the first agent who showed us nice homes in an area we would like to live in and that were also close to the university. He showed us two houses that were both a little above our price range to buy (besides we had no jobs). One house had a nice large open living and dining room area with a fireplace. These houses were in an area which, priced today, would cost from $300,000 to $400,000. John was very impressed with the house. I was not particularly impressed and wanted to continue to look. That night, I dreamed about the house, and afterwards, I had that special knowing in my heart that the Lord was revealing that this was the house chosen for us. When I mentioned this to John, he felt that perhaps we were expecting too much and it was not within our price range. Still, for some reason, I was convinced that this was the house. So I prayed, "Lord, if this is the house for us—the one you want us to have—please give John the faith and the wisdom to know how to get it." Now, John didn't know that I had prayed this prayer, and about a week later, after he had attended a prayer meeting, he came home shouting, "Gloria, I know how to get the house!"

The Lord had spoken to John as he drove from the prayer meeting, telling him to purchase the house by putting down $2,000 and making an agreement to buy it six months later. The Lord had given John the wisdom and the faith. When I look back on this, it is amazing, because we did not know this was known as a lease/purchase agreement. We prayed, and John called the real estate agent. He told him that the Lord had revealed to him how to get the house. The real estate agent responded by emphatically stating, "I've told you before, John, the owner does not want to rent the house." John responded, "Are you working for him or for me?" The agent said, "For you." The agent called the owner again with the plan the Lord had given us, and the owner agreed. A week later, we moved into the house, but we still did not have jobs and needed to qualify to get a mortgage for the home. In spite of this we believed that God had spoken to us, and because we were obedient to face the challenge, God's word to us would be fully manifested.

Before we left the Horner's, something wonderful happened. While we were preparing to leave Delaware to come to Tulsa the second time, I took our youngest daughter, Christina, to the doctor's office for her regular exam. At the end of the exam, the doctor explained that Christina had a hernia, and we should take her to the doctor once we got to Tulsa.

One night, after being at the Horner's home for about three weeks, we were awakened by Christina's crying as if something was hurting her. Very concerned, John picked her up from her pallet on the floor and began to earnestly pray for her as I looked on, praying silently. We knew why she was crying because we could feel and see the hernia protruding. Then John lifted her up to the Lord and prayed, "Lord, I cannot heal Christina. If I could, I would, but I know You can." After a few more minutes of prayer, Christina became quiet and John placed her on the pallet to continue sleeping. From that day forward, Christina never cried again, as if the hernia was hurting her.

About a week later, I made an appointment with the pediatrician in Tulsa and took her for an exam. The doctor carefully examined Christina, and then indicated I could put her clothes on. As I proceeded to do so, I was perplexed that the doctor said nothing about the hernia. I knew I had to ask him, just to be sure. I told him that the doctor in Delaware had told us Christina had a hernia, and we should have her checked when we arrived in Oklahoma. He immediately had me to remove her clothes again, and again he examined her. He then said, "I can't find anything." From the time we prayed for Christina to this very day, she no longer had any pain or protrusion in that area of her body. We know that she received a miracle of healing, unexplainable, but very real.

It seemed, particularly at that time, that we never ceased to be in need of a miracle. We were now in our home in

Tulsa, but we needed jobs to secure a loan to purchase the house. While John went to class, I prepared to go to the Tulsa Board of Education to apply for a position. This was at the time of year when most teaching positions had been filled. Two months after moving into our home, I went to the school board and completed an application. In April, I still had not heard from anyone regarding a position. By that time, John decided that it would also be good if he applied for a position. One morning after we prayed, John decided to go directly to the school board to apply for a teaching position. When he walked into the building, a man standing in one of the doorways saw John and asked, "Why are you here?" John responded that he was there to apply for a science teaching position. He added, "I have not completed an application, but my wife has completed an application for a teaching position in music." The man asked what my name was, went over to a box of applications, and found my application at the bottom of the pile. It just so happened that this man was the assistant superintendent of the school district. As soon as he saw my application, he instructed John to have me to call him as soon as possible. I called and was immediately given an appointment and sent to two school principals for interviews. After an interview at the second school, I was hired by the principal to teach piano lab. I am still amazed at how God directed and guided John to go to the school board that particular day and how a person who had the authority to hire was there at the very moment John walked into the building.

Indeed, God blessed us. I knew I had a position, but one was still needed for John. Both of us needed jobs to qualify for the mortgage. While John was going to school, he also continued to apply for positions, but nothing seemed to come through. It was now July, and we had only about a week left to qualify for the loan. Otherwise, we would lose our down payment on the house and have to move. We earnestly prayed for a miracle. The real estate agent called to find out if we had qualified for the mortgage loan. John informed him that he was still looking for a job. John then said to the agent, "Ask the owner to give us an extension of one week." The agent replied, "John, didn't I tell you that the owner does not want to rent the house?" Without hesitation John again replied, "Who are you working for, me or the owner?" The agent replied, "You." He then told John that he would go to the owner and get back with him later. We breathed a little easier when the agent called and informed us that the owner had consented to an extension of one week only. Without a doubt, we needed a miracle, or we would have to move. We had peace that in spite of our circumstances, God was with us.

Several days of the next week passed; still John did not have a job. On the day before the day we needed to finalize the loan, John took our son John to the Catholic school he attended. While there, he spoke to Sister Mary, telling her he needed a teaching position. Sister Mary asked him about his educational background and informed John that there was a science position open at Bishop Kelly High School and he should call Brother Thomas about the position. After talking to Brother Thomas, John was really excited. The next day, which was Friday, he went to interview with Brother Thomas. John needed a salary of $15,000 to qualify for the loan. This was also the last day we had to get to the bank and let them know we had the needed additional $15,000. To our amazement, John was hired on the spot without review of his application. He asked Brother Thomas to write a letter stating his salary of $15,000, the exact amount needed. John hurried from the school to the car where I was waiting, and we rushed to the bank with the letter, barely getting there before the bank closed. John entered the bank with proof of his teaching job; when he came out, we had been approved for the loan. What a miracle!

The Miracle of Receiving the Holy Spirit and the Call

Years earlier, John and I had witnessed the great magnificent power of God that began to be manifested in our lives after we became aware of the presence and power of the Holy Spirit. For me, the Holy Spirit is a Person who manifests the love, presence, and power of God. When I was about six years old, I accepted Jesus Christ as my Lord. Some people say that children do not understand enough to be able to accept the salvation of God, but I noticed a difference in my life from this early age. From the time of asking Jesus to come into my heart, I found it very difficult to tell a lie, and I felt that I could pray and the Lord would really hear me. I remember having a great desire to read the Bible and wanting to attend and be a part of Sunday school.

From this young age, I felt the protection of my parents and of God. But after marriage, three children, and the stresses and complexities of life, I felt like something was really missing in my Christian walk with God. To try and find out what was missing in my life, I began to read the Bible again. As I did so, I became more and more aware of the miracles Jesus performed while he walked on this earth, I began to more and more wonder why we did not see such miracles happening in our own lives and in our church.

At the time, John and I were both Catholics, although previously I had been a Baptist. Years later, my father became a Baptist minister in addition to being a college professor. I wondered if miracles still happened in this day and time. It appeared that God must have heard my thoughts. One day as I drove John, Myrtle, and Jacqueline to Catholic school, I heard a minister on the radio talk about the healings Jesus had performed through his ministry. I never heard such talk in the Catholic Church I attended. In fact, one Sunday while in Mass, the priest during his sermon seemed quite dejected. He talked about visiting a parishioner who had cancer and revealed that he did not know what to do. Having now heard, as well as read, how Jesus healed the sick as he walked this earth, I boldly went up to the priest. I say boldly because this is something I never would have done previously. After the service, I asked him why didn't he pray that the person with cancer be healed. He responded that this was not a part of his seminary training, but he knew of a group of people who did believe in healing. They were David and Teresa Maguire. I called this couple and was invited to their next prayer meeting.

The prayer group was made up of persons of various denominations—Catholics, a Pentecostal, and even a Presbyterian—who met in the Maguire's home. They prayed to Jesus as if they knew him personally, and this is what I wanted—the reality of Christ in my life. They also talked about being baptized in the Holy Spirit. Seeing how real the Lord seemed to be in their lives, I asked them to pray that I be baptized in the Holy Spirit. I had previously asked the Lord to let me know in some way if this was what I should do. At the third meeting I attended, they talked and read Scriptures pertaining to the Holy Spirit and I felt in my heart, without a doubt, that I should ask them to pray that I be baptized in the Holy Spirit. I had asked John to attend the prayer meeting with me, and he was also present. After the meeting, they gathered around me, placed their hands on me, and prayed that God, in the name of Jesus Christ, would baptize me in the Holy Spirit. As they prayed, I felt a special love and warmth I had never experienced before. My response to this experience was to go around the room and hug each person. I just felt a special love for everyone there. John, seeing my response, decided that he wanted to be baptized in the Holy

Spirit too. John must have noted something different about me because the next week he decided that he would ask to be baptized in the Holy Spirit. Everyone graciously prayed for John, but afterwards, John was very quiet. Even as we drove home, he had very little to say. It appeared that nothing happened as a result of our prayers for John. But one early morning hour, something special did happen.

Receiving the Holy Spirit (in John's words)

"One morning I was suddenly awakened by a very hard rain. I could hear the pounding of the rain on the roof, and as I listened, I began to think about God's wonderful creation and all the things that the rain provided for—water to wash with, vegetations to grow, and drink for various living creatures all the way down to the smallest microscopic organisms. Suddenly, the rain ceased to make noise on the roof and was transformed into the most beautiful sounds I had ever heard. I could hardly believe my ears; it was breathtaking. There are no earthly sounds ever produced that can match the melodies this rain produced. God had planned an unforgettable experience that rainy morning. God's divine rain was like a beautiful symphony that gave my heart and spirit an indescribable peace. All I could do was to give praise to God's name. This is when I came to the realization that something different was happening, and I felt the presence of the Lord. I was suddenly moved to confess my sins, and I said, 'God, please forgive me for keeping you out my life so long.' As I said this, I began to feel waves and waves of God's Spirit flowing over me, in me, and through me. I had never felt so alive in my life. The presence of the Lord was astoundingly real. Then I saw my arms being lifted up. I looked at them with great curiosity because I was not consciously lifting them up, but I knew that it was right. It was like a complete surrender to God's will for my life. I then heard myself praising God and thanking Him for His love and forgiveness. I knew that I was saved, and I knew that all of my sins had been forgiven.

"My heart was filled with so much joy that I now came to realize what Christ meant when he told the woman at the well, "*'whoever drinks the water that I will give him will never be thirsty again. For the water that I will give him will become in him a spring which will provide him with living water and give him eternal life'* (John 4:14 GNMM). What a wonderful God and Savior! What peace and joy They bring! As I praised the Lord, in my own language, I found the words that I was saying inadequate to what I really felt within. Exhausting every word in my vocabulary in giving thanks and praise, I then found myself speaking in an unknown tongue, and I knew that it was right. I knew that I was now praising the Lord in a way that was equal to what I felt within. I had received the gift of speaking in a new language that expressed my love to God.

"During the entire time that I was experiencing the wonderful presence of the Lord through the Holy Spirit, my wife, Gloria, was sleeping like a lamb. After what seemed an eternity, I began to cry very quietly because I didn't want to disturb Gloria, nor did I want her to disturb the Lord and me. Nevertheless, she did awaken and began to ask me what was wrong. By this time, I was experiencing the enfolding, infilling, and overpowering anointing presence of the Holy Spirit, an experience that, even now, I cannot fully explain in words. I heard Gloria speak, but I could not express to her what I was experiencing. As tears streamed from my eyes, Gloria was beginning to get worried and a little frightened. After all, she had never seen me cry and the expression on my face caused her to think I was in pain. As she later described it, my face was completely changed.

"Gloria kept asking me if I was in pain. To the best of my ability, I tried to tell her I was not in pain. We had a pretty hard time communicating with each other, so she decided to call a doctor. As you know, three a.m. is a difficult time to try to reach a doctor. Having no other choice, she left a message with a doctor's call service.

"Before the doctor called, I had another unusual but wonderful experience. A very loud and audible voice called my name, 'John.' For some reason, I answered, 'Yes, Lord.' The voice continued, 'Do you love me?' Again I said, 'Yes, Lord.' The voice continued, 'Do you love me?' Again I said, 'Yes, Lord, I love you.' The voice said, 'Feed my sheep.' 'Yes, Lord,' I said, 'I will feed your sheep.' A second time the voice called, 'John, do you love me?' Again I said, 'Yes, Lord, I love you.' Then the Lord said with more authority, 'Feed my sheep!' I said, 'Yes, Lord, I will feed your sheep.' Then a third time the Lord said, 'John, do you love me,' and a third time I answered, 'Yes Lord, I love you.' The voice continued, 'Feed my sheep!' This time I knew by the authority in the voice, I was to make a promise to feed the Lord's sheep. So I said, 'Lord, I promise to feed your sheep.' (When the Lord spoke to me, there was no thought that this was the way He had spoken to Peter. It has always been perplexing to me that the Lord spoke to me in the same way. When I discussed this with a spiritual friend, he strongly felt that this was God's call and anointing on my life.)

"As mysteriously as the voice came, it went away. During this time, Gloria was at a loss as to what was going on. We have a custom of reciting the Twenty-third Psalm when there is a crises or an unusual situation. Doing this in past situations had brought us much peace and comfort. Gloria, as she had done in other situations, began to recite this psalm. As I began to recite it with her, it was not my normal voice we heard. The voice which we heard sounded about an octave lower than my regular voice. It sounded like a seventy-eight-speed record being played at thirty-three-and-a-third. The sound of my voice was very slow, much slower than any speaking voice my wife or I had ever heard. In spite of the strangeness of the sound, Gloria continued to speak the Twenty-third Psalm; as usual, it brought us peace.

"Suddenly, my face returned to its normal state, and my voice became normal. It was over. Gloria and I looked at each other. She was happy that I looked and spoke like my usual self again, and I was happy for the wonderful experience of the Holy Spirit. *Boy,* I thought, *if anyone tells me that our Lord is not alive, I'll not believe it!* Now, I knew that all the talk I'd heard about God being dead proved to be empty words. Those who believe this are being deceived. It is clear this is what Satan wants humankind to believe, so he can rule over us without any opposition.

"The doctor returned the call, and Gloria was relieved to tell him I was much better—quite an understatement. He suggested she call in the morning if I did not improve. I was much more than improved. In fact, this experience confirmed my salvation! Jesus had answered my prayer; I had experienced the gift of the Holy Spirit. Although I was an active Catholic and attended church each Sunday, this was my first personal experience with Jesus through the Holy Spirit.

"Since that rainy morning my life has never been the same. I thank God for sending His Son into the world to die and rise from death for me; I thank God that what little intellect I have been blessed with did not stand between God and me; I thank God that I did not allow pride to keep me from the light of God; and finally, I thank God for helping me open up my heart and mind completely and willingly. Because of this, I have a deeper relationship with God the Father, God the Son, and God the Holy Spirit. What a joy this has been in my life. The fullness of the Three Persons of God cannot be fully comprehended or appreciated unless they are experienced in both the heart and mind.

"This experience of being baptized in the Holy Spirit is quite unique and few people experience such overwhelming power in the beginning, as I did. When Gloria was baptized in the Holy Spirit, she experienced a very peaceful, warm, and electrifying feeling. When I initially received prayer to be baptized in the Holy Spirit by the members of the prayer community which I attended, I did not feel or experience any manifestation at the time. In fact, this very real manifestation of God's Holy Spirit did not occur until about two weeks later. I remember feeling disappointed and discouraged because there was no outward manifestation of the Holy Spirit. This may be part of the reason God's presence was made known to me in such a real and unusual way. Still, I realize now that we should not feel this way if we do not see any sign or manifestation.

"Never be discouraged if you do not experience an immediate manifestation of the Holy Spirit when you first pray and ask to be baptized in the Holy Spirit. The manifestation will come later. Just continue to have faith, praise the Lord, and look forward to the Spirit with great expectation. Remember that all things work for the good to those who believe and love God.

"Several nights later, I was awakened by the Lord at 3:00 a.m. and these words were spoken to me: 'Rise and be joyful in my name. Sing and be joyful in my name. Dance and be joyful in my name.' I didn't understand why I should do this, and furthermore, I saw no reason to sing, dance, or be joyful. Still, I realized that I must be obedient. I decided to get up so I would not wake up Gloria.

"The closest room was one that we used for an office. I began to do exactly what the Lord told me. Though I felt very awkward and stupid, I attempted to dance and be joyful unto the Lord. Suddenly the Lord said, 'Stop!' As I stopped, the Lord said, 'John, I have called you from the foundation of the earth. I have called you to teach and preach the Gospel of the Lord Jesus Christ, to go from east to west. You will pray for the sick whom I will call to you.' Then the Lord said, 'Open your mouth. I'm going to put my words in your mouth.' As I opened my mouth, something that felt like spittle touched my tongue, and God spoke in a language I did not understand. The Lord then said, 'Stretch out your hands. I am anointing your hands to heal the sick whom I will call to you.' I felt like something was moving from hand to hand, which I later realized was the Holy Spirit. Silence fell on the room, and I broke out into singing, dancing, and praising God. Now I really praised and really sang and really danced unto the Lord. This went on for quite a while. I was having a Holy Spirit time in the Lord all by myself. Then it all made sense what God said initially. Hearing directly from the Lord and knowing what God truly wanted me to do was another miracle."

Two

Christ, the Giver of Salvation and King of Miracles

Jesus just didn't talk God's love; he acted in God's love and he demonstrated God's love. Because of his love for God and his love for humanity, he delivered those who were overcome by the evil one, healed the sick, and preached the Good News of the kingdom of God. Jesus proved that God's love never fails, even as he was being put to death on the cross. God's love would not allow him to remain in the grave, but God raised Jesus up as the first of many sons and daughters to live eternally with God. Jesus said there is no greater love than the love of one who lays down his life for his friend, and truly that is what Jesus did for us. In fact, if you were the only person, Christ would have died for you. No mere words can describe the love of God for each of us and what Christ did for us on the cross so we could be forgiven of our sins. Christ redeemed us with the shedding of his blood and made it possible for us to have new life and a healed relationship with God. If you knew how much God loves you, your heart would always be filled with joy and peace because you would know that no matter what you are going through, God's love is always here. This love defeated death and sin and continues to live on, not only in the heart and mind of God and Jesus Christ, but in the power of the Holy Spirit. It is for us to believe and receive God's loving grace, which we call salvation, a new life through Christ.

God's goodness, love, and mercy have been given to us in the form of what we know and experience as salvation. It is God's way of healing the broken relationship caused by the mistrust and disobedience of Adam and Eve. Most importantly, salvation is God's gift of love and mercy. It is God's greatest gift to humankind. If we are concerned about our spiritual health and wholeness, this is the first gift we should receive towards that wholeness. Our relationship with God is most important to the wholeness of our spirits, our bodies, our minds and our relationships with others.

As humans, we have proven time and time again that we are unable to live righteous and holy lives within our own strength and power. (We just can't say no.) If we look at the history of our world, we see constant strife, division, war, and inhumanity to one another. We need a higher source of power to enable us to be people of love and compassion. We need a higher source of power to free us from those emotions that destroy our personal relationships. We need a higher source of power to overcome those things that make us sick in mind, body, and spirit.

In salvation, we are delivered from those things that cause strife and disharmony in our relationship to God and others. We are given God's grace to be set free to love; we are set free to forgive; we are set free from those emotions of guilt, anxiety, resentment, anger and deep hurts that not only destroy relationships but lead to sickness and disease. The origin of the word *salvation* comes from the Greek word *sozo,* which means *save* and is often translated in English not only as salvation but as healing, health, and wholeness.

It may also be translated to mean liberation or deliverance. Jesus came to restore us to the wholeness that God always wanted for us from the beginning of creation. Jesus came to heal our brokenness that kept us separated from God. The salvation of God through Jesus is not only healing for the spirit but healing for our bodies, our minds, and our relationships. Jesus came to heal us in every way we are broken and most importantly to free us from sin, guilt, and spiritual death.

In salvation, God's image is renewed in us, and we are transformed into a life of holiness and righteousness. God, through Christ, not only delivers us from sin, but Christ is the Great Physician. John Wesley, the father of Methodism, emphasized prayer as a means of direct healing and recognized the interrelatedness between physical and spiritual wholeness and between the mind and the body. He affirmed and understood healing to be of both soul and body and his understanding of salvation was holistic (Maddox, *Responsible Grace*, pp. 146-147).

Jesus demonstrated this connection between the spiritual need for salvation and the body when he healed the paralytic who was brought to him by his friends. When Jesus saw their faith, he said to the paralytic, *"Take heart, son; your sins are forgiven"* (Matt 9:2; Mark 2:5; Luke 5:20). In the Gospel of John, Jesus healed the man who had been lying by the pool of Bethesda for thirty-eight years. When he saw the man later in the temple, he told him, *"See, you have been made well! Do not sin anymore, so that nothing worse happens to you"* (5:14 NRSV). Still, when he healed the blind man, Jesus made it clear that there are also those who have not sinned and are sick. In John 9:3, the disciples asked Jesus if it was the sins of the man or his parents that caused the man to be born blind. Jesus answered, *"Neither this man nor his parents sinned; he was born blind so that God's works might be revealed in him*" (NRSV). The disciples had asked this question because they, like the scribes and Pharisees, believed that sickness was God's punishment for sin and disobedience. This concept was developed in the Old Testament.

But Jesus came to do a new thing, and he had a purpose in performing the works of God. He revealed that God is a God of love and compassion and is present to those who love Him. When Jesus healed people, he did not ask these persons what they had done or tell them that God was trying to teach them something. Instead, he healed them first, and if they had sinned, he told them to "go and sin no more." Jesus, as Luke points out, came to set us free from those forces from which we cannot protect ourselves. Once we are set free by Jesus, he empowers us to stand strong, not in our own strength, but in the strength of God.

In addition, Jesus placed great importance on the works of God that he performed. We see evidence of this when John sent two of his disciples to question Jesus concerning whether or not he was the expected *"one who was to come."* Of all the things Jesus could have made reference to, he chose to reply. *"Go back and report to John what you hear and see: The blind receive sight, the lame walk, those who have leprosy are cured, the deaf hear, the dead are raised, and the good news is preached to the poor"* (Matt. 11: 4-5; Luke 7:22). Jesus also made clear the importance of the miracles he performed when he said, *"Do not believe me unless I do what my Father does. But if I do it, even though you don't believe me, believe the miracles"* (John 10:37-38b).

Jesus not only was a great worker of miracles, but before he left this earth, he gave his disciples authority to do the works of God in his name. In John 14:12-13, he said, *"I tell you the truth, anyone who has faith in me will do what I have been doing. He will do even greater things than these, because I am going to the Father. And I will do whatever you ask in my name, so that the Son may bring glory to the Father."*

Miracle in Classroom 211 (in John's own words)

"Jesus promised, *'And whatever you ask me in my name I will do, so as to glorify the father in the Son. Anything you ask in my name I will do'* (John 14:13-14 NAB). The students of classroom 211 have seen the fulfillment of this and other promises given us by Jesus, the Son of the Living and true God. This experience will always be treasured in my heart and in the hearts of the students who lived it. At the time, I was a seventh grade teacher of General Science at Burnett Middle School.

"It all began as a result of the formation of a photography club as a special interest class. In faith and as a believer in the promises God has given us, I set out to organize the photography club with no available funds or materials. Officers were elected and the age-old struggle of obtaining funds sought us out as its victim. What I did not realize in the beginning, when the photography club was formed, was this was the will and purpose of God. Let me again emphasize the fact that none of us had any idea where we would get the funds or support for the club. We were going to simply trust in God to supply our needs.

"First, the school had no available funds to support the programs already in existence, let alone a new one which would add to the overstrained budget. Our state government had mismanaged or over-calculated its revenue earnings and was now having to make up for these mistakes. The schools were left with very little or no extra funding for extracurricular activities.

"In faith, we decided not to let this deter our efforts to have a photography club. We decided that each day for one minute at the beginning of class, we would pray silently, asking God, through Jesus Christ, to supply our needs in establishing and maintaining the photography club. We began the prayer session on a Monday in October. We continued to pray, and no one seemed to openly object to the idea although some displayed an air of reluctance. (This was a miracle in itself.) On Tuesday after our period of prayer, I proceeded to teach some of the high points of photography, our involvement in it, and some of the benefits of such a club.

"Photography was a new experience for most of us. Nevertheless, we had set our course and looked ahead to the Lord as our All in All. On Wednesday, I was inspired to talk to the principal, Dr. Dillon, to see if some funds had suddenly become available, and if so, would he assist the photography club in its financial dilemma. To my surprise, he was very enthusiastic and responded to my request with twenty-five dollars for the club. Every atom of my being rejoiced. Oh, the joy of the Lord in my soul was overflowing! All I could think was, *Praise, God! Praise, God!* This was the beginning of many wonderful ways in which the Lord met our needs. The hand of God was at work, and God proved to be a promise keeper. I thanked both the Lord and Dr. Dillon for the twenty-five dollars.

"Edward Maltose was the next person to become involved in God's will and plan concerning the photography club. Mr. Maltose and I met for the first time at the Lincoln Camera Shop where he was a manager. When I entered the camera shop, a dark-haired, bearded man approached, asking if he could help me. I responded, 'Yes, but allow me to look around first.' There were so many wonderful and interesting articles attracting my attention. By sight alone, the twenty-five dollars was spent many times over, and still I knew it would be impossible to get the club off the ground.

"Finally, I motioned to the nice gentleman that I was now in need of his expert service. It was apparent that he was very knowledgeable about the merchandise and the operation of the camera shop. Most of the other salesmen turned to him for advice or to help them make the final judgment about a certain sale.

"Before going to the camera shop, I asked the Lord to go before me to make all the necessary decisions and arrangements. After meeting Mr. Maltose, it seemed as though he and the Lord had gotten together to talk over my arrival and my needs for the club. I told Mr. Maltose that I knew very little about photography but, nevertheless, had formed a club in my school. I explained that there were few activities in the school to interest our youngsters and perhaps the photo club would solve some of the problems. I requested that he select the necessary materials and equipment to get the club started, all of which would cost no more than the twenty-five dollars I had in my pocket. He went about, very seriously selecting materials for the club. Whatever the Lord spoke to him was certainly more than what I prayed for.

"When he finished, he put the articles on the countertop. After a quick appraisal, I priced them to be in the amount of fifty to sixty dollars. My thoughts were racing. Did he hear me clearly when I said I only had twenty-five dollars, or did he fail math as a student? Then he said, 'I think this will do it. I believe you can get started with this.' I thought, *Boy, if I can't, don't look for me to come back to your shop for help again*. Mr. Maltose continued, 'That will be ten dollars.' My only thought at this moment was to give him the ten dollars as fast as possible, before my hearing returned to normal or before he realized this big error.

"Praise the Lord! My hearing was normal. I heard right, and the salesman knew full well what he was doing. The problem was with me. The Lord was teaching me that he was true to his promises in the past, he was true to his promises at that very moment, and would also be true in the future. 'Lord,' I said, 'you really keep your promises and answer prayers. Not only that, Lord, but you accept challenges of a school teacher and his students.' My limited vocabulary was not enough to thank and give praise to my heavenly Father and His Son, Jesus. So, I used the prayer language God has given me to give praise and thanksgiving.

"Oh, what a wonderful Lord we have. All we need to do is believe and trust God with all our hearts and minds. This was the lesson I wanted to teach my students, yet I was still learning myself. The next day, I brought out all of the photography equipment for my students to see. To see the joy in their eyes and the smiles on their faces was enough to convince me that this was the lesson the Lord wanted to teach them also. It was truly a happy and joyous day for us all. We discovered that we had developing tanks, developing and fixing solutions, film, trays, sponges, and an electric lamp—all the things we needed. We were now prepared to take pictures, develop the negatives, and make contact prints. We could hardly wait to get started.

"For all of my students, this was a new way to see their loving God and our Savior, Jesus Christ. My personal love and faith in God was greatly increased. This was one time I was glad I stepped out in faith. Now I believe without a doubt that God always honors the faith one places in our Lord. *'We have this confidence in God: that He hears us whenever we ask for anything according to His will'* (1 John 5:14 NAB). *'Yet he must ask in faith, never doubting, for the doubter is like the surf, tossed and driven by the wind'* (James 1:6 NAB).

"What my photography class learned and what the world should know is *'God, with all His abundant wealth in Christ Jesus, will supply all your [our] needs'* (Phil. 4:19 GNMM).

God is not limited, and no need of ours is too large or too small to be met. All we must do on our part is to believe. God will do the rest. Many times, we do not receive the abundance of wealth God has for each of us because we will not accept the Word of God in its simplicity. The students did not need any further encouragement after seeing this blessing. Their hearts were overflowing with the joy of the Lord. Now when I asked the class to pray, immediately everyone bowed their heads, and no one showed any hesitation or doubt.

"Later, the power of God through the Holy Spirit worked again in a special way. A professional freelance photographer was invited to come to Burnett Middle School to give a talk and show some of his works to the photography club. This was the result of the efforts of Mr. McMullan, a friend and science teacher. Remarkably, the professional photographer and Mr. McMullan could pass for brothers. They looked and dressed similarly. Before Mr. Schmitt departed, after giving an enjoyable, enlightened talk concerning photography, he told us he would send some useable equipment he was not using. We thanked him for everything and resumed our regular routine.

"About a week later, Dr. Dillon stopped me in the hall to tell me he had a new camera kit for the photography club. Immediately I thought the kit was from Mr. Schmitt. I was amazed to discover that it was a donation from the Lincoln Camera Shop. Then, in about two weeks, Mr. McMullan came to my room, carrying a large box packed with equipment. It had been given to us by Mr. Schmitt. He too had kept his promise, sending two cameras, film, developing tanks, light meters, a timer, safety light, blotter pads, and many other useful items. If we were excited before, words could not describe our feelings after this.

"Our God is a God of great love and surprises. God never tires of giving. God wills to show us great mercy and deep concern for our well-being and happiness. I have come to know that our Lord has a wonderful sense of humor. I have the sense that it pleases the Lord to make our life a little easier and just a little happier than we ourselves imagine it to be. The students in classroom 211 were so thankful and grateful to our loving God and God's Son.

"All of these blessings made lasting impressions in the hearts and minds of each member of the photography club in classroom 211. Many had come face to face with our blessed Savior for the first time. Now we could boast about Jesus. Through this reality, many came to know Jesus more personally. At least these fifty students could never entirely deny the existence of the One I call my Master and Savior, Jesus. We give God all the glory and praise.

"Our progress in learning photography was growing rapidly. We had learned to develop very sharp negatives and good contact prints. Our next goal was to learn how to make enlargements. One problem was we did not have an enlarger. By now, I was confident that we would obtain an enlarger before the next school day. This was in fact a promise I made the students. After making the promise, I thought, *Lord, where will the enlarger come from?* At this point, my confidence in the Lord was unshakeable. I said a short prayer and thanked the Lord for providing an enlarger.

"When I arrived at Lincoln Camera Shop, Mr. Maltose greeted me and offered his service. 'I need an enlarger for the photography club,' I said. 'I am shopping for an inexpensive one, or a used one, we may be able to pay off, either by the sale of photos or little by little.' He walked over to the shelf where the enlargers were located and began to inspect them for price and quality. Then he picked up an Omega model and handed it to me. He said, 'You can have this one; it will cost you fifteen dollars to replace the lens.' At these words, I replied in excitement, 'Is that all? That's terrific!' *Oh dear Lord,* my heart sang, *thanks, thank You so very much.* Mr.

Maltose was the instrument through which God blessed the photography club. Again, our Lord proved God answers prayers and is true to God's promises.

"I went back to the school as fast as the speed limit would allow. Carrying the enlarger, I rushed into Dr. Dillon's office with a large smile on my face. 'We have an enlarger!' I exclaimed. 'All I need is fifteen dollars to buy a lens. Just think, fifteen dollars and we will have an enlarger.' I don't know if I made sense to him, but when I finished, he asked if I wanted cash or a check. 'Either way,' I said.

"Mr. Reeves, the vice-principal, was in the office at the time and made several remarks concerning the possibilities of the enlarger. After we all made several verbal exchanges, Dr. Dillon suggested ways to earn money for our future needs. He suggested that I take over sponsoring and managing the school portraits project that was used to raise funds for special school activities. Dr. Dillon explained that the previous year, the project netted the school six hundred dollars. If I would take over the running of the project, the photography club would be given half of the earnings.

"The lens was purchased, and we were now in business to raise working capital for the club. The success of the club progressed far above anyone's expectations, and the quality produced was, in a word, beautiful. We received many compliments from every teacher on the staff. Many more students expressed an interest in the club and paid to have their own portraits made.

"Many thanks, as we have expressed in so many ways, go to our loving and generous God and Jesus, our Brother and Savior. What can be said? How can we ever give thanks to our God? It is impossible to out give or out love God. All we can do is thank God and believe in God's Son, putting our complete faith and trust in them. *'Whatever you ask for in prayer with faith, you will receive'*" (Matt. 21-22 NAB).

Three

Miracles of Healing

George Frey—Healed of Pleurisy (in John's words)

"*The Spirit of the Sovereign Lord is upon me, because the Lord has anointed me to preach the good news to the poor. He has sent me to bind up the brokenhearted, to proclaim freedom for the captives and release from darkness for the prisoners, to proclaim the year of the Lord's favor*' (Isa. 61:1-2; Luke 4:18-19). These words were spoken to Isaiah, the holy prophet of God, and proclaimed again by Jesus who fulfilled these things in accordance with the Scripture. Jesus had revealed the good news of salvation and the benefits that those who believe would receive. The following testimonies reveal that Jesus continues, as he did two thousand years ago, to fulfill this Scripture through the power of the Holy Spirit:

"George was one of the dearest and most mature Christians I've known. The love of the Lord was written on the expression of his stern face. His life was dedicated to being a servant and disciple of the Lord. Through our common love of Jesus, the Living Son of God, we became very close. I had adopted him as my earthly spiritual daddy.

At the time, he was of the Pentecostal faith, and I was of the Catholic faith.

"This testimony is about George and the miraculous way Jesus Christ intercedes for us at the right hand of God. From our very first acquaintance at a prayer meeting held in the home of David and Teresa Maguire, I knew God's hands were on this man. The things we have shared in the Lord could be a complete book; but for our purpose here, we will share his story.

"As a result of a car accident, George had to undergo several operations. Since the operations, his body had not regained its normal strength. His body could not withstand the demanding hours and physical abuse he had to endure. In the late fall, during a time set aside at our prayer meeting, George requested prayers for his illness, stating that he was having severe pains in his side, suffering from shortness of breath, and tiring easily. As customary, members of our prayer community gathered around and laid hands on George. In the New Testament, Jesus foretold one of the signs that would follow those who believe, *'they shall lay hands on the sick, and they shall recover'* (Mark 16:18b KJV). The most prevalent spiritual gifts manifested in our young prayer community, as in other charismatic groups, were speaking in tongues and prophecy. Only a few members had received these gifts in the prayer community. Most of these persons, including George, had received the baptism of the Holy Spirit before joining this particular prayer community.

"We had prayed for the gifts of the Spirit, and I suppose we were anxious for the manifestation of the gift of healing because of the many requests for healing. A week or two had gone by, and the community continued to believe George would be healed. There were many more requests for healing as we continued to grow in faith and to grow as a prayer community. The Spirit of God was certainly at work in our community and in the lives of many of its members. Our hearts and minds were being opened to the Word of God and the power of God. Jesus was becoming more and more alive in us in a very real way. His presence was strongly sensed, and many of us were opening up to God's love. Strangely, I was experiencing a need to pray more. There was a noted change in my prayer life after being baptized in the Holy Spirit.

"Other things were happening in my life and in Gloria's life. We were reading book after book concerning the Holy Spirit and attending various functions to learn firsthand about the power of the Holy Spirit. We attended Reverend Jim Brown's services at the Upper Octorara Presbyterian Church in Parkesburg, Pennsylvania and the Full Gospel Business Fellowship Banquet meeting near Lancaster, Pennsylvania, once a month. At one of these meetings we heard a prophecy that a person attending would become a student at Oral Roberts University. One speaker, Dr. Howard Ervin, was a professor at ORU. Later, I became a student at ORU in the School of Theology, fulfilling that prophecy. George and his wife, Dorothy, had invited us to attend the banquet. However, on that occasion, George's illness prevented him from attending.

"George continued to experience difficulty in breathing. Sometimes he was barely able to speak due to the severe side pains and the shortness of breath. He was forced to speak at a whisper. We were very concerned about George's health. My heart was very sad; we hoped that God would touch him in a very special way to make him well and whole.

"We later learned that George was suffering from a condition known as pleurisy, an inflammation of the pleural membrane of the lungs. This condition caused George much discomfort. Due to the nature of his work, he was constantly exposed to wet and cold weather, and he had to work long and hard hours as an auto mechanic. Sometimes he would work nine or ten hours a day under these conditions. He was on his feet and required to do a lot of walking during most of these hours. The combination of adverse conditions, plus his physical weakness, made George a very sick man.

"After his condition worsened, George's doctor ordered him to bed for a week. The doctor's diagnosis showed that George's condition was due to pleurisy and high blood pressure. While under the doctor's care, George rested at home, but with little relief. He was unable to sleep or get the proper rest he badly needed due to a stitch-like pain in his side from a sitting or lying position. Only his faith in God gave him any hope or relief.

"God does answer prayers. It happened on Monday, March 13, 1972, at about 6:30 a.m. As I stood praying by the kitchen window, the power of God's Holy Spirit came over me like rippling waves, beginning at the top of my head, passing through my body, and continuing down to my feet. As the Spirit fell upon me, I immediately began to pray for George. My prayer was not of me; there was something supernatural about it, as though I was standing there listening to what was being said.

"A great power and authority came from my lips. Words were spoken that I dared not speak on my own authority. The Spirit of God used me as His vessel. I was chosen and given the confidence and wisdom of a divine revelation that George was at that very instant being healed. In my heart and mind, I knew God had spoken to and through me, and God had given me the knowledge that George was healed. Afterward, I repeated over and over, "George is healed. George is healed." My heart was filled with joy; in a deep and sincere way, I praised God and thanked God for His Son, Jesus, in whose name we claim all healings.

"Immediately, I shared this experience with Gloria, and together we thanked and praised the Lord Jesus and our loving God. Gloria and I then prayed for discernment to know the will of the Lord. We then agreed to call George and share the good news.

"Dorothy answered the telephone. Remembering that St. Paul said that all things must be done decently and in order, I spoke as calmly as possible. I said, 'Hello Dorothy, how are you this morning?' She replied, 'Fine, how are you?' I then asked, 'How is George?' To my joy, Dorothy answered, 'He woke up this morning and said that he felt fine, and the pain in his side has gone. He felt well enough to take a shower.'

"Finally, I explained what had happened a few minutes earlier. I told Dorothy that God had revealed to me that George was healed. She said, 'Praise God!' Then I went on to tell her how the Holy Spirit had come upon me, interceded for George, and commanded that he be healed and made whole. At that, she called George to the telephone.

"When George came to the telephone, I said, 'George, you are healed. God has healed you.' For about five minutes we did not speak about the healing; we simply praised and thanked God. Our hearts were overflowing with the love and joy of the Lord. He answered our prayers and healed our brother in Christ. After telling George all that I had experienced, he confirmed the healing. God showed us that He is true to His promises and honors the faith of His children.

"This was one of the first major healings manifested in our prayer community, giving us cause for great rejoicing. God had proven again God's love and power, both of which are without limits. Through the grace and mercy of God, George was restored to perfect health. Later, George went to the doctor who could not find anything wrong with his lungs, stating that his high blood pressure was also normal. He told George he could return to work the following Monday.

George could once more enjoy the pleasure of normal breathing, and he could sleep normally because there was now no pain in his side. As Kathryn Kuhlman would say, 'When God heals you, you are really healed.'"

The Healing of George's Friend, John
(John P. refers to John Penn)

George had asked John P. several times to go with him to pray for his friend John. John, a much older man, was in the hospital, unable to move or talk. John P. had a difficult time matching his schedule with George's so they could go together to the hospital. One day while John P. was teaching a tennis class, he whispered a prayer to the Lord concerning praying for John at the hospital and expressing that he was ready to go. As soon as John P. prayed that prayer, rain started pouring. John took this as a sign from the Lord that he was to go and pray for John. What was unique about this is that it was only raining on the tennis court. John P. dismissed the class and got into his Volkswagen to go home. As he drove, it seemed the rain was following him. When John arrived home, he called George to see if he was available to go and pray for his friend. He was, so they agreed to meet at George's. As John P. traveled to get George, the rain intensified. As they headed to the hospital, the rain came down extremely hard. George prayed that God would hold back the rain, and immediately the rain subsided. They were surprised that George's prayer was answered so quickly. Praising the Lord, they quickly entered the hospital and walked to John's room.

John was sitting in front of the television, watching *Gunsmoke*. After greeting John and introducing John P., George explained that they were there to pray for his healing. John was unresponsive. In the meantime, the nurses passed back and forth, looking into the room to see what they were doing. George told John that he and John P. were going to anoint him with oil, lay hands on him, and pray for his healing. John's situation was very serious; he was motionless and unable to speak. The doctors did not give him any hope of walking again or being able to remember anything from his past. As George and John P. spoke to John, he never responded to what was going on around him. He stared straight ahead at the TV, showing no signs of hearing George and John P.

John P. anointed John, and both men laid hands on him; then John prayed a very simple prayer of faith that God would heal him. After they prayed, John P. and George conversed a little while, then left. There was no sign that their prayer had been answered.

The next day, George called; his voice was filled with great excitement. He told John P. that when the nurse tried to move John back to his bed, his body moved. The nurse was so startled she almost wrenched her back, knowing that previously he never made a move and always remained in one position.

"Day by day, George reported to John P. about the changes occurring in John's body. Little by little, John was regaining the ability to move on his own. Within days, George reported that John was not only able to move, but was making progress in his ability to walk and talk. He was also remembering things about his past. John was eventually released from the hospital. This is a unique` example of a miracle happening over an extended period of time.

The Healing of Our Son Mark
(in the words of John and Gloria)

The birth of our son Mark fulfilled a dream for Gloria and me. As a young married couple, we dreamed of having a family of four children, two boys and two girls. Mark was the completion of our dream. However, this was a decision we made before we knew the Lord as we presently do. Today, we no longer have this attitude; it would be the Lord's will we seek concerning our family and its size.

Before Mark was born, the doctors were concerned about the baby's weight because they thought he would be born two months prematurely. The doctors feared that a premature birth could cause a weight problem which, in turn, could contribute to other abnormal conditions. The doctors were not in any way encouraging early labor though there were signs of such; nevertheless, Mark arrived early.

After delivery, the doctor explained that our new son was much larger than was expected. He told us that, in spite of this, the baby was small enough to be placed in an incubator for protection and observation. Aside from his small size, the baby had jaundice, a yellowing of the eyes and skin. This condition, as explained by the doctor, had something to do with the baby's blood, and tests would have to be made to determine the exact cause and whether a blood transfusion would be necessary. In spite of these complications, Mark was a fine-looking baby boy.

Gloria and I put our trust in God to heal Mark and correct the problem with his blood. We believed in our hearts that if God can create life, He can also maintain life. It seemed as if God had prepared us for such a circumstance. We were not alarmed by the report of the baby's condition; we were confident that a blood transfusion would not be necessary. We prayed a simple prayer of faith, asking God, in the name of Jesus, to heal Mark without a blood transfusion being necessary. We simply believed our prayer would be answered. We believed the Scripture to be true, that we could ask anything in the name of Jesus, God's Son, and God would grant it.

There was no immediate change in the baby's condition. Each day the doctor's report was the same. The condition did not worsen, nor did it improve. Finally, after several days, the level of the jaundice gradually began to lower. There was no need for a blood transfusion; there were no complications. When we heard this good news, we praised God and rejoiced in the name of our Lord Jesus. God had given us victory over sickness, and we were victorious in the Lord. Right then and there, God showed us that God not only answers prayers of healing, but nothing is impossible for God. Again, God was glorified. God was showing us that He knows no such thing as defeat. God honors the faith of every believer.

Later, a small hole was discovered in Mark's heart, a congenital heart defect. The doctor encouraged us not to worry because Mark was not showing any signs of discomfort or negatively reacting to the condition. He emphasized that he did not see any real complications, and Mark was doing well. He expressed that Mark's overall appearance and response were pleasing.

Though we as normal human beings were very concerned, our hope and trust were in the Lord. We did not understand all the reasons behind these things; we knew all things happened for a purpose. We were happy that we were growing in the Lord and could find peace in God. Gloria and I had come to the place of trusting God. If no one else could, we knew in our hearts and minds that through Jesus, our Father God would and could heal Mark and make him whole.

According to Scripture, *"To everything there is a season, and a time to every purpose under heaven: A time to be born, and a time to die; a time to plant, and a time to pluck up that which is planted; A time to kill, and a time to heal"* (Ecc. 3:1-3 KJV). God had chosen a time to reveal God's power and greatness as Divine Healer and Great Physician. Not only had God chosen a time to heal Mark, but He had chosen to do it in a most remarkable and miraculous way. Jesus himself would glorify the Father.

Miracles of Healing

One night, as I was sleeping peacefully—like most normal people, between the hour of two and three a.m.—the presence of Jesus awakened me. Somehow, by divine revelation, I knew Jesus was present in my bedroom. Several times before, I had experienced the real presence of Christ, and usually I would awaken to see if I could see or listen quietly for him to speak to me.

This time, the manifestation of the Lord's presence was stronger than ever before. No matter how one would attempt to explain or describe one's personal experience with the risen Christ, words are hopelessly inadequate. All one can say is he knows it happened and it is the most thrilling and important experience in one's life. After an experience with the Lord, our Savior, one is never the same. There is always a supernatural change which takes place in one's life. Perhaps in this day and time, many wonderful revelations are being experienced by those individuals who believe in the risen Christ and seek a personal relationship with the risen Christ.

After the strong presence of the Lord was manifested, a great peace came over me and a strong compelling urge to listen for his voice. In that moment, the Lord spoke. He said, "Get up and pray for Mark." At this, I sat up slightly, to hear His voice more clearly. Again the Lord commanded, "Get up and pray for Mark." Then I had a vision. In the vision, the Lord was standing by the crib where Mark was sleeping. A third time, the Lord commanded that I get up and pray for the healing of Mark.

The vision was very clear. I was able to clearly see the Lord standing by the crib, leaning over the rails with his hand upon Mark's body in the location of his heart. As the Lord commanded, I got out of bed and went into Mark's room.

In faith and obedience, I laid my hand on the spot where Jesus placed his hand on Mark in the vision. As I did so, Jesus imposed his hand onto my hand. As I began to speak forth the prayer of faith for Mark's healing, something very unnatural occurred. All at once, a strange sensation took place in my body. From the top of my head to the bottom of my feet, a warm rippling or wave-like sensation passed through my body. When this sensation took place, I had a sense of great power and authority. Aside from these supernatural manifestations, the Lord, through the power of the Holy Spirit, prayed an intercessory prayer by way of my mouth, That is, the prayer I vocalized was not prayed under my own authority but by the authority of Jesus Christ. This power and authority were manifested by the workings of the Holy Spirit.

There was so much power and authority in that prayer, I knew it could not have come from such a lowly person as me. Only Jesus could pray such a prayer. Only Jesus has been given such authority from God. As I opened my mouth to pray, this intercessory prayer came forth: "I am the Lord thy God and have heard your prayers. I am the healer of the world. Be made whole and perfect. Rise in my name. This was part of my plan from the beginning of time—you were to be healed. Rise and be made whole and perfect. You are healed in my name."

As strangely as it began, it ended. During the entire experience, I felt the anointing power of the Holy Spirit. At no other time prior to this had I ever experienced such a manifestation of the presence of Jesus. Since this experience, God has continued to bless our family through other supernatural gifts and manifestations. Though there have been other experiences of Jesus, through the Holy Spirit, this experience will always be a special blessing for Mark and our family.

This manifestation of the presence of Jesus has made a definite impression on my mind and heart. Even today, I hold this as a special experience and anticipate knowing more, concerning the wonderful works of the Holy Spirit.

For many years, we did not see the manifestation of Mark's healing, and we wondered how one could experience the presence of Jesus and yet, have no proof of it. One day, Gloria heard about a young girl who was not able to play with other children or participate in any activities because of a hole in her heart; at times she even had to be carried from place to place. When Gloria heard this, she rejoiced in the healing of Mark, though it was not physically manifested. Mark is one of the strongest of our children and has always been able to run, jump, or do any physical activity he desired. While in high school, he participated in sports without any problem. So, it really made no difference whether his heart physically appeared to be healed or not. Not only this, Mark was one of our healthiest children; he was very rarely sick, if at all.

Recently, Mark was examined by a doctor who determined that he had a heart murmur. But the doctor told him, "If it hasn't bothered you all of these years, don't worry about it." Mark has been a blessing beyond expectation. He is special to every member of the family. Because of him, we have learned many wonderful and vital lessons concerning faith and trust in the Lord Jesus. We have surrendered to the Lord every problem or complication, known and unknown, concerning Mark's health and well-being. It is through faith in Jesus, our High Priest that God's love and promises are manifested. We must live by faith in all circumstances. *"Do not, then, surrender your confidence; it will have great reward. You need patience to do God's will and receive what He has promised"* (Heb. 10:35-36 NAB). We have learned that we walk by faith and not by sight.

The Healing of Our Son, Stephen

When Stephen was born prematurely at seven months, we knew that we had witnessed another miracle. He was well formed and in good health though he had to stay in the hospital until he was five pounds and also had a little jaundice.

After Stephen stayed in the hospital for about two months, we were really happy to take him home. His older brothers and sisters very much enjoyed having him home and thought he was the cutest baby they had ever seen. They all wanted to hold Stephen and take care of him. As Stephen developed and grew larger, we could see that he was very intelligent. We had just one concern—his feet turned in to the point where the larger toe on each foot overlapped, and they were not becoming naturally straighter.

As any concerned mother would do, I took him to the pediatrician and explained my concern. The doctor suggested that we wait a few months longer and then take him to a children's hospital to have him fitted with special shoes to be worn for perhaps several years. We were very concerned, so John and I didn't just wait during those few months. We began to pray as we waited, massaging his little feet and praying on a regular basis that they would begin to straighten out from the ankles. After doing this for one-and-a-half to two years, we began to see a difference. It was a gradual process, a response to continuous prayer.

About the time Stephen started to walk, we could see that one foot had almost completely straightened out and the other foot was still slightly turned in. We continued to pray, and we encouraged Stephen to try and walk with his feet turned in a straighter direction. By the time Stephen was seven or eight years old, there was very little sign of his feet having been anything other than straight. Later, as a teen, Stephen became a cross-country runner in high school and to this day, he runs five to ten miles on a regular basis. A few years ago Stephen participated in the Peach Tree Marathon. It was quite a joy to see him run so well, he achieved his personal best. Some miracles happen over time, and we should, in some instances, continue to pray until we witness the complete healing. Some have called this "soaking prayer." Believing that all things are possible gives us motivation and comfort not to give up, for with God all things are indeed possible if we persevere and wait on the Lord.

God Cares about Little Things—Gloria

God is not only concerned about the large things that happen in our lives; God is also concerned about the small things. Following is an account of my experience with God's healing grace:

One morning, I awoke to find a sore on my finger. Thinking that perhaps I had been bitten by some insect and it would soon go away, I thought no more about it. Later, it grew more painful and filled with pus. There also appeared to be a wart next to the sore on my finger. Remembering that Jesus is the Great Physician, I decided to pray about it. I did pray and truly believed that the Lord could heal me. The sore continued to grow in pain and became more filled with pus until it was twice its original size. The wart remained beside it. Still, I believed God would heal me. But when three days had passed, I was becoming quite concerned. The spirit of fear was creeping in, and I began to think I was quite foolish for not going directly to the doctor.

Quite fearful by now that something dreadful was happening to my finger, I talked with John about it. I expressed that perhaps my prayers were not good enough and someone else should pray for me. John explained with much authority that Jesus was the healer. It didn't matter who prayed or whether I was of a denomination that believed in divine healing. All I needed to do was to believe and have faith.

Although I was not quite convinced, I decided that I would pray about it and also pray about whether or not I should go to the doctor. After praying and asking for a confirmation from God, I opened the Bible. Immediately, my eyes fell on these words: *"For you are all sons [and daughters] through faith in Christ Jesus. For as many of you as were baptized into Christ have put on Christ"* (Gal. 3: 26-27 NKJV). I do not know what happened to me as I continued to read, but somehow I realized that God was saying to me that if other persons could ask in prayer to be healed and they were healed, I could do the same. I realized that I did not need to go to anyone for this particular healing; all I needed was faith in Christ Jesus. God is no respecter of persons to those who believe. Even more, I knew I was healed.

Even though my finger looked no better, there was no doubt in my mind that I was healed. I took a shower and for the first time in the past few days, I had no fear of pain from placing my finger in water. As the water ran over my finger, I rejoiced, knowing I was healed and there was absolutely no pain.

I believe God allowed this to happen to teach me patience and to let me know that, no matter what appeared to be happening, He was always with me. It was truly a great lesson for me. Even though a doctor could have relieved the pain, I never would have experienced the joy and the glorious experience of God's grace and love. Though God works through doctors to heal us, when God heals directly, the healing is always perfect. There was no after pain or a scar from the removal of the wart had I gone to a doctor. In recent years, God healed me of a large cyst as I took Holy Communion. This healing also left no scar. Previously, I had two cysts removed from my shoulder by a very fine doctor; years later, the marks remain from the removal of the cysts.

God's direct healing, through Christ, was and is perfect in every way. My faith grew tremendously from this small and important experience. I feel that I am better prepared for any larger problem that may occur.

The Miraculous Healing of Earl Chandler

In the first chapter, I wrote about our trip to ORU and how the Holy Spirit confirmed God's guidance that John should become a student. After three years, John completed a master's degree in theology, and we returned to live in Newark, Delaware where we began to attend Holy Family Church. To our delight, this church also had a prayer community which included vibrant worship and teaching. We attended along with about fifty people. At one of these meetings, John and I observed an African American man come in; he was barely able to walk and his back was bent over. His wife, Kim, who was of Asian background, brought him. She had been attending the prayer group for some time.

During the meeting, one of the leaders asked us to take this man to the sanctuary to pray with him. We found out his name was Earl Chandler. The four of us, Kim, Earl, John, and I, entered the dimly lit sanctuary and walked toward the altar rail. While standing before the altar rail, John and I laid hands on Kim and Earl and began to pray. Almost as soon as John began to pray, Kim, to my amazement, quietly fell to the floor under the anointing of the Holy Spirit. We then began to pray for Earl and again, to our amazement, Earl immediately went from being bent over almost to his waistline to a straight upright position. Of course, we all rejoiced in the Lord and the powerful healing/miracle that was manifested.

Later Earl told us he had been in the military and while participating in a karate tournament, a contender had given him a death kick in his spine. Because of this encounter, his vertebrae were crushed. From that moment on, Earl had not been able to stand erect. He was discharged from the Army and could no longer work.

Several days later, Earl called John, expressing that he was beginning to have some of the same symptoms he had before his healing. John responded by telling him that he must stand firm in the Lord and on God's promises. He said, "If you knew a thief was coming to your house, would you just open the door and let him come in?" Earl replied, "No." John explained that Christ said, *"The thief comes only to steal and kill and destroy. I came that they may have life, and have it abundantly"* (John 10:10 NRSV). He told Earl that God would not heal him and then take the healing back; it was the enemy who was trying to steal away his healing so God would not be glorified. He must resist, as Scripture says, and "the devil will flee." From that moment on, Earl never had any more problems and continued to walk with a straight back.

Some months later, he gave testimony of picking up the back of a Volkswagen with no pain or any ill effects. There seemed to be just one problem. Now that Earl was healed, he wanted to get off disability, but when he went back to the doctor, they found that his X-ray looked exactly the same, his vertebrae still looked crushed. The doctors had no explanation for why his X-rays looked the same, even though he could stand upright without pain. Earl could bend and do all of the things that a person with a normal back could do. Still, they refused to approve his being taken off disability. About two years later, the doctors were convinced that his back was indeed healed, and Earl was able to discontinue receiving disability. God, indeed, does work in mysterious ways. We cannot limit God to how he chooses to perform miracles!

The Miraculous Healings of the Silankas Family

About two years after John and I were baptized in the Holy Spirit, we began to attend Holy Angels Catholic Church. There was no prayer group in this church community, so John decided to ask the priest if we could begin a prayer community that would include teaching and worship. Shortly after our request, the priest consented to our starting a prayer group that included an hour of teaching.

John was teaching on the importance of the Holy Spirit in our daily lives. After the fourth session, two young teenage boys of the Silankas family asked to be baptized in the Holy Spirit. This family lived in the neighborhood where we had lived for a short time and had just begun to attend our prayer community.

As John began to explain how he was going to pray, something most unexpected happened. The Holy Spirit came upon John and the children, even before he began to pray; John experienced the presence of the Spirit going through him like rivers of living water. John realized there was something that the Spirit wanted to do and had the distinct discernment that someone there was sick, yet no one appeared to be sick. When John asked the three children if they felt the presence of the Spirit, they replied with an emphatic "Yes!" John had a strong discernment that the Holy Spirit's presence was available for healing. He then asked, "Are any of you sick?" Vincent said, "No, I'm not sick, but my brother Ricky is." When John turned around to look at Ricky, blood was flowing profusely from his nose.

Later, John learned that Ricky had a history of chronic nose bleeding. John laid his hands on Ricky's head, while blood was streaming from his nose. As soon as John did so, the flow of blood immediately stopped. When the bleeding stopped, Vincent began to laugh, in excitement. John asked Vincent why he was laughing since there appeared to be nothing funny. Vincent informed John that Ricky's problem of nose bleeding never stopped before unless his nose was packed, and they often had to go to the emergency room to get medical assistance. After praying with Ricky, John discerned that the presence of the Holy Spirit, with its powerful anointing, was leading him to pray for each child present, so he laid his hands on Vincent and prayed for him, as well as Ricky, even though Vincent did not appear to have any physical problem.

While Ricky went to wash his face, John continued to pray for the other children. Meanwhile, I had gone downstairs, then came back up to see why John was taking so long to come down to the prayer meeting. Vincent and Ricky informed me that Ricky was healed of a nose bleed. The Holy Spirit truly intervened in the lives of these children.

John and the children went downstairs to share this joyful news with the others in the prayer community. Everyone began to thank and praise God for the marvelous healing miracle, but this was not the end of the story. While downstairs, we prayed for Carmelita, their mother, and Richard, their father; both were healed of back pain. Later, as we were leaving to go home, John and I prayed in the parking lot for Richard's salvation.

Later we discovered that God had performed an additional miraculous healing. One Sunday morning, the Silankas family went to Howard Johnson's. While waiting to be seated, Vincent was drawn to look at postal cards on the rack, some of which were 3D. Vincent began to look at them one by one. He was amazed because he had never been able to see in 3D before. Barely able to contain his excitement, he told his family that he could see objects behind one another in the 3D cards. Vincent was excited because he had been born with no depth perception and crossed eyes. The doctors had cosmetically corrected his crossed eyes, but they could do absolutely nothing concerning the depth perception. Vincent had never been able to play baseball or catch because of this lack of depth perception. The family was elated with joy. A few weeks later they took Vincent to have his eyes checked. The doctor's examination proved that Vincent's eyes had been healed and he had perfect vision. The correction of Vincent's vision confirmed and medically proved that the discernment given to John was not misplaced, that Vincent was indeed healed as John prayed for them to be baptized in the Holy Spirit. It was clear that Jesus not only baptized the children in the Holy Spirit, but miraculously healed them.

These miracles of healing teach us that God loves us and is present to us. God is not some distant god who doesn't care about our trials and tribulations. God is concerned that we be in good health and is concerned about our spiritual, mental, and physical well-being. God only wants to do us good and not harm. To reveal God's love and power, God sent his Son, Jesus, to be a deliverer to us from the attacks of the evil one. Jesus was and is a deliverer from physical, mental, and emotional suffering, pain, and guilt. He was given authority to heal and make whole those who would believe and receive. Jesus, in turn, has given us that same authority. In fact, to this day John continues to teach that the Church is a healing community. This is confirmed by the Scripture that says, *"I tell you the truth, anyone who has faith in me will do what I have been doing. He will do even greater things than these, because I am going to the Father. And I will do whatever you ask in my name, so that the Son may bring glory to the Father"* (John 14:12-13). This miraculous intervention of God in the healing of Ricky and Vincent, and even more, baptizing them in the Holy Spirit, truly brought glory and still brings glory to God.

The Healing of My Back (Gloria)

Ephesians 6.10 reads, *"Finally, be strong in the Lord and the strength of his power"* (Ps. 138:3 NRSV).

When I look back at the times in my life when I saw the mighty hand of God move in a powerful way, they were in those times when I was willing to take a risk, to step out in faith, to face the challenge and depend on God to be my strength.

One such time came years ago when I awoke with sharp, continuous pains in my head. This was a shock to me, to say the least. I immediately woke John and told him I needed to go to the hospital. Not only was I having sharp pains, I couldn't sit up. When I told him, John's immediate response was, "You will not have to go to the hospital. I'll pray for you." Now, years later, John does not remember saying this. After some thinking about it, I believe he said this under the anointing of the Holy Spirit because in normal circumstances John would have immediately taken me to the doctor's office or the hospital emergency room.

The pains were so sharp I could barely lift my head, and I had to literally roll myself out of bed onto the floor and crawl to the bathroom. Something inside me would not let me give up. I felt I had to move, I had to walk, and I had to fight boldly. I had to do something to show I was trusting in God, and God gave me the strength to do this. Not only did John's support give me the strength to fight for myself, but the strength of the Holy Spirit, God's power, was there to comfort, to encourage, and to guide me in how to pray.

As I stepped out each morning in faith and trusting God, God gave me wisdom, boldness, and courage to fight and believe until my healing was complete. It all sounds so simple here, but it was not. Each morning I would struggle to get up, praying for God to give me the strength to raise my head and get out of bed. As I took each step of faith, more strength would come. Once I was able to stand up, I walked around the house reading the Psalms, including Psalms 23, 91, and 103. I would proclaim these words aloud throughout the morning. As the Holy Spirit showed me what might be trying to overtake my body, I took authority, in Jesus' name, over each infirmity or disease that would come to mind. Finally, on the fifth day after the attack, I began to thank and praise God that I was healed. Sometime during that week, I called the doctor to make an appointment for the following Monday. But all glory goes to God, because I was healed by Friday of that week. When the doctor examined me on Monday, he could not say for sure what I had experienced because I was completely healed. He thought perhaps it might have been an arthritic attack at the beginning of my spine.

At least thirty years have passed since that attack on my body. For the first few years, I would often feel a tinge of pain in the area behind my neck next to the top of my spine, but I would immediately take authority and command the pain to leave. The pain would go away as soon as this prayer was said. In the past over twenty years, I have felt no pain in that area. But the enemy of our souls doesn't give up; he constantly tries to attack in some other way. Thanks be to God, through God's Son, Jesus, we have the power to overcome and walk in victory.

When I stop to think about what gave me motivation, impetus, or encouragement to start the healing process in my body, it was prayer. First the prayer of my husband, John, then, strengthened by his prayer, my own prayers, prayers of spiritual warfare, and finally prayers of praise.

Four

Prayer and Miracles

The foundation of miracles can be found in our relationship to God and our faith in God's power and faithfulness. The prayer that moves the heart of God toward showing us the miraculous is the prayer of faith. *The prayer of faith is based on the Word and the promises of God. It is the prayer that is lifted up in trust in God's power and might, not our own. It is a prayer spoken from the heart of one who believes in God's righteousness and faithfulness.* Jesus said if we abide in him and his Word abides in us, we can ask anything we want and it will be done by the Father in heaven (John 15:7). God is faithful to hear us, but we have a responsibility to love our Lord, believe his word, and obey the commands of Christ. We cannot do these things on our own; we need the Holy Spirit. Then we can pray with expectancy that God will hear us and will answer us. When we abide in Christ, we are enabled to pray prayers of faith and have full confidence in a living God who hears us, answers us, and cares for us.

Just exactly what does it mean to abide in Christ? Abiding in Christ requires that we have a relationship with God. This relationship in turn requires communication. You wouldn't think of having a relationship with your friend, your husband or wife, or anyone else in complete silence. One of the joys of having a friendship or relationship with someone is being able to communicate and share our deepest thoughts, our joys, our fears, and those things that connect our lives. One way we understand how to communicate and relate to God in Christ is through God's Word and the teachings of Christ. So, in order to pray and communicate effectively with God, we must have some understanding of God's Word in Christ. In addition, the Holy Spirit is of utmost importance in enabling us to abide in Christ, to understand God's Word, and to communicate with God.

Many people know very little about prayer because they have done very little concerning the study of God's Word. Through study, speaking, and proclaiming the Words of God in Christ, we are able to create an environment and a place where we communicate with and relate to God. I say "in Christ," because Christ said that all authority in heaven and earth has been given to him. In turn, Jesus in his authority gave authority to the disciples, saying: *"Therefore go and make disciples of all nations, baptizing them in the name of the Father and of the Son and of the Holy Spirit, and teaching them to obey everything I have commanded you* (Matt. 28:19-20a). When we know God's Word, we can speak God's Word, proclaim it in the midst of adversity, and bring down those strongholds that stand against us and others. From the Old Testament to the New Testament, we have been given precious nuggets to direct us in our communication and relationship with God.

The power of prayer is beyond what we can think or imagine and its benefits are beyond measure. Some benefits of prayer include:

1. The assurance of God's presence
2. Peace of mind—a peace that surpasses all understanding

3. Fullness of joy
4. A sense of completion and wholeness in our relationship to God, in Christ, and a sense of well-being.
5. Being able to see the difficult situations we are in from God's perspective. When we see things from God's perspective, we come to understand that we need not fear the situation we find ourselves in. God is in control.
6. Relief and release from stress
7. Receiving revelation, discernment, understanding, wisdom, and knowledge by communication through the Holy Spirit
8. Preparation for perilous times.
9. When we pray we find refuge and strength; we are able to stand in the midst of trials and tribulations.

The importance of praying the Word of God is to assure that we are praying in the correct way. When we consistently pray, using the promises of God, we are building our house on a solid foundation. When we pray the promises of God, we not only provide an atmosphere for our prayers to be answered, we open the door for miracles to happen when we pray for ourselves and intercede for others.

One of the most remarkable miracles we have witnessed as evidence of Christ's promise that the disciples would be able to lay hands on *"sick people, and they will recover"* (Mark 16:18) happened when we lived in Tulsa. John had been asked to teach one session on the Holy Spirit at a small Catholic Church. The people enjoyed the teaching so much, they asked us to come back for several weeks. This gave us an opportunity to get to know the people. After a few weeks, we invited those who attended the teaching to our home for an evening of fellowship. Everyone had a great time, and at the end of eating our potluck dinner, we decided to have a time of prayer. John placed a chair in the center, so that if someone wanted to have prayer, they could sit down and we would gather around, place our hands on them, and pray. Much to our surprise, our two year old daughter, Christina, jumped into the chair. Everyone just laughed, and John asked, "What can we pray for Christina?" Immediately, I thought about the times I tried unsuccessfully to get her to use the potty, so I said, "Pray that she be potty trained." Again, everyone laughed, but John quickly led in prayer that she be potty trained. Just as quickly as Christina jumped into the chair, she jumped out of the chair.

The next person we prayed for was a nine-year-old girl. Her mother asked that we pray for her feet because she had never been able to wear street shoes. She had to wear high-top tennis shoes because her ankles were weak and she walked with her feet turned in. As John led in prayer, he held her feet and ankles in his hand. Then a most remarkable thing happened. Her bones began to shift and move in John's hands, not once, but several times. He could feel her bones shifting and moving. When the movement stopped, her ankles were like any other child's ankles. The next morning she was able to put on street shoes, something she had never been able to do before. Her mother had saved those shoes and told her that one day she would be able to wear them. What a miracle, an instantaneous correction of her feet! To top it off, God did not forget my concern that Christina be potty trained. The next day and from that day on, Christina went to the potty without any problems. Sometimes, it seems our Lord is just waiting for us to ask, and is there in an instant to grant our request, no matter how large or how small.

Another important aspect of prayer and healing is to pray with compassion. Years ago, when we were attending a prayer group in Tulsa, one of the attendees was a man who had one leg much shorter than the other, causing him to have a prominent limp. Each time I saw him, the thought would come to me that we should pray for him. One day, I got up the courage to ask to have prayer for him. The prayer group consented and John and I led in prayer. We prayed, but the man's leg looked the same. Afterwards, the thought that I was not led by the Holy Spirit in asking for prayer was constantly on my mind. About two months passed before he came to the prayer group again. He informed us that from the time we prayed for him, he had no more pain in his leg. For years after being seriously injured in a car accident, he had been taking from fourteen to sixteen pills a day for pain. Now, since that time of prayer, he had no more pain. Just think, if we had not prayed, the man would have continued in pain. It was the compassion of the Lord that motivated me to ask that we pray. I often wonder what would have happened if we had continued to pray. Perhaps he would have no more limp. Sometimes we need to use what is called "soaking prayer" for God's miracles to be manifested. Praying just once is often not enough; we need to continue to "soak" the person in prayer.

Jesus performed many miracles because of his compassion, love, and concern for others. He was a person of compassion with action. Among other things, the compassion of Jesus moved him to feed the hungry (Matt. 15:32); to teach the lost (Mark 6:34); and to heal the sick (Matt. 14:14). Let us too allow the compassion of the Holy Spirit to move us into action.

Five

Testimonies: Miracles of Healing

The Healing of Gloria Bovankovich (in her words)

Another amazing healing that we witnessed firsthand is that of Gloria Bovankovich. Gloria had multiple sclerosis. Following is her testimony:

"After thirteen years of having M.S., the disease struck me hard and left me completely paralyzed on the right side, from head to toe. There was no mistaking that I had M.S. In fact, the doctors considered the case to be taking a typical course. To add to our concern while in the hospital, tests confirmed my suspicion that I was pregnant with my fourth child. Prayers were already flooding heaven for my recovery. I learned quite definitely that my will power alone (and I was once very proud of it), no matter how strong, could not move even a toe on my stricken foot. I didn't know whether I'd ever be a wife to Carl again, whether I'd ever pick up my tiny boys again or be able to hold that baby not yet born. I had to leave everything in God's hands. I gave back to Him those cherished gifts: my beloved husband, my children, my body, my very self.

"How gentle and kind is the Lord! Through all this troublesome time, He surrounded me with people, and through them, I recognized His love assisting and sustaining me. And He began to heal me. I went home with a wheelchair and a walker. Gradually I walked again by myself, and the use of my hand and body returned. By August, I was well on the way back and little Paul was born healthy and whole. How we thanked the Lord!

"In the early part of 1972, the Lord led me quickly through various events and experiences to bring me to an important point in my life. I attended a Bible study group during Lent, and the discussion was of miracles and the faith that precedes them. I began to go to the prayer meetings at the Newman Center. It was like walking into the New Testament. I rejoiced to find people who enjoyed praising God and who loved to talk about Jesus. Through them, I began to learn more about faith and healing. The healing of a body was just a small part of what God was to give me. I received the baptism of the Holy Spirit. I began to praise God in a strange tongue. Early one morning while in silent prayer, a thought came to me that I knew was not mine. I took it for the voice of the Lord. Clearly, He said to me: 'I don't want to take you from your family; I want to give you to them.' I knew immediately that God would cure me of M.S., completely. Along with this certainty came a gentle conviction. It was I who had been keeping myself from Carl and the boys. Right then, I told the Lord I no longer wanted to keep myself from others, but to serve them, and in this way, serve Him. I wanted Him to heal everything in me that kept me from giving of myself. At the prayer meeting on May 3, 1972, I asked the community to pray with me for healing. As we sang and praised the Lord, I became spastic, shaking and jerking all over. I'd had spasms like this before as a result of stress, but usually I was able to hold them off until alone. But that night, I abandoned myself to God—to work in me as He willed. About five of the members led me into another room. Carl had to help me; I could barely walk. They laid their hands on me as I half reclined in a chair, jerking and twitching. As they prayed, the nervous spasm disappeared. It started in my feet and moved through my entire body—a profound quiet. I was peaceful, but tears were streaming down my face. I knew that I was cured then and there, cured of an incurable disease. Jesus had done it as He promised. Praise His holy name! I walked back with the others to the main hall where the rest of the community was singing. And then, I danced, really danced for joy!"

(Gloria Bovankovich's healing from the author's perspective: That night, as we usually did at the Newman Center, we gathered together to pray for our weekly prayer session. John and I remember the joy that came over Gloria's face after being anointed with oil by John and the five of us laying hands on her as John led in prayer. She jumped out of the chair and ran around the large room where we were, something she had not been able to do for years. We were simply amazed at what God had done.)

Gloria continues, "Since that night, I've become stronger as time passes. A few symptoms remain—a prickling sensation in my face, occasional weakness in my leg; but I am confident these too will disappear when God wills. Three weeks ago our family returned from a vacation at the seashore. I recalled my earlier refusal to go anywhere with them, but I went and returned, happy and strong. I have new energy and stamina. I've suffered no setbacks with M.S."

Author's Note: Gloria remained free of M.S. for eleven beautiful years. We don't understand why, but after that time, Gloria again had the symptoms of M.S. But, we do know that during those eleven years, she was able to take care of her family and see all of her children become young adults. She traveled from place to place and witnessed to many concerning God's healing love and grace in her life.

Healing of Donna Rust (in her words)

In the spring of 2011, John and I were invited by Pastor C. J. Hill to his church, First United Methodist Church of Canton, to give teachings to those interested in learning more about the gifts of the Holy Spirit. Near the end of those teaching sessions, one of the faithful attendees, Donna Rust, asked us to pray for her. Following is her account of healing:

"I met Revs. John and Gloria Penn a couple of years ago during a class I took with them on the spiritual gifts. At the time, I was having lots of problems with my left foot. I had been in a lot of pain for quite some time and found it hard to walk without limping or using a cane. I just knew if I went to the doctor, I would be faced with surgery and a very long healing period. Not to mention, I did not have medical insurance. Reverends John and Gloria Penn both prayed to God to heal me from my pain. Within a few days, I was no longer in any pain, and to this day I am walking fine with no pain! Praise the Lord! I know firsthand God's love and healing powers.

"Now on another note, I know God answers our prayers in the way he sees fit. I was laid off from work and pushed into early retirement. I thought this was the worst thing that could happen to me. I was devastated, to say the least, since my husband had just started his own company and we were living off of my income. Our grown son, who was also living with us, was unable to work and having major problems with his back and leg. Shortly after I was laid off, our son had to have surgery on his leg and almost lost it; he also had major back problems. For the next year, I spent a lot of time with him while he was in the hospital for his back and leg surgeries. When I was not at the hospital, I was blessed with lots of odd jobs cleaning homes to bring in some money. About a year later, my son died. God knew I needed this time with him. I was comforted to know I did everything I could for him and was able to spend the last year of his life caring for and loving him. Times were hard, and my son was not the best patient, but God kept me going. I was at peace when he passed away because I knew he was in Heaven and no longer in pain. I thank God every day for our blessings."

Headaches: No Match for the Power of God
(in Eleanor Allen's words)

The following is a healing miracle I requested from Mrs. Eleanor Allen:

"My aura, defined by Webster Dictionary as a disturbance in vision, is movement as if looking at flowing water, first at the periphery, then increasing until the entire visionary field is involved. Meanwhile a stabbing, throbbing pain starts in my left temple. Sounds echo in my head. Lights hurt and nausea starts. I will be having a migraine headache.

"I had learned to close my eyes at the first sign of wavering vision, turn off all sources of sound, and take a pill. If I was not able to take measures, the condition could last up to three days, and I would not be able to drive, go to work, or complete household chores. I would lie in my bed, in a darkened room, with a cold cloth on my head and my left hand pressing my left temple.

"Sometimes fatigue or stress aftermath would set off the headache, sometimes nothing. For many years I had only rare occasions, but now they were increasing in frequency and severity. My physician, Dr. Yadav, prescribed Maxalt and gave me some samples to try. They worked, but I had to rest until the relief came. I carried them faithfully in my purse because they had to be taken at the first aura sign. When I went to refill my prescription, I was shocked at the cost! My friendly pharmacist recommended a lower cost replacement called Imitrex. They worked, but not as well.

"One day, while working as a Registered Nurse in the operating room, I felt an aura starting. I got my new prescription, but delayed taking a pill because of the "sleep effect" it might cause. I tried to finish the case, but within the hour I was unable to correctly complete my paperwork. I was relieved by another nurse. Because this was an unusual event, I was taken to the Emergency Room. Several injections were given to me, and I was referred to a Dr. Drexinger, a neurologist, and sent home with more prescriptions (Compazine and Fiorninal).

"I continued to have a series of headaches with the auras. When I mentioned this to my friend, Gloria Penn, she told her husband, John. They both came to my side right then and prayed with me for the relief of my headaches. I had immediate relief, the wavery "water effect" lifted, and the throbbing and pain in my left temple subsided. It was like taking off sunglasses when entering a tunnel! Thankfully I proceeded with my life.

"I first became aware of the Penns when Gloria Penn suddenly became unconscious during a church service. She was carried out to the foyer to lie down. The whole time, her husband John Penn was earnestly praying for her. We nurses checked her for signs of physical damage. There were none. She regained consciousness and was later checked by her physician and cleared. I credit John Penn's prayer for influencing a good outcome to the problem. Reverend Penn is an influential teacher at the Allen Temple Church. He and Reverend Gloria Penn had been co-teachers of the Gifts of the Holy Spirit class which my husband and I had attended. Both have a great understanding of the Bible and how to allow the power of the Holy Spirit to work in prayer to heal people.

"Several weeks later, Gloria asked how I was doing. I said I was somewhat better, but that some headaches were still happening. She immediately called her husband over, and together, right there in the church parking lot, they began to earnestly pray for my relief and healing from the headaches. My head filled with a glowing white light, and the pressure was lifted!

"Now, many months later, I have not had another migraine headache. The last two of my Maxalt tablets are still being carried in my wallet. They will expire soon, and I will never use them!

"I, Eleanor Allen, am a Registered Nurse. Most of my fifty-year career has been spent working in the operating room. I tend to be factual and exact, especially in matters of the body. I have been a nutritional consultant for twenty years; therefore, I understand many of the effects upon the body of diet, pollutants, and lifestyles. I was raised in the church. The Bible has always had a strong influence in my life. Spiritually, I am trying to grow and to become a better Christian. I know that in my career, I have been able to help many people, but in a minor way. Even when I volunteered in other countries, I was only a part of the team. I am in awe of the power of God, as written in the Bible, and of the Spirit of Jesus Christ. I am in awe of the Penns because they have been able to use this power throughout their lives to help others. I thank God that they were able to use the power of Christ to help me!"

(*Author's Note:* John and I declare, to God be all the glory for the things God has done.)

The following miracles are given by two ladies I have met with, prayed with, and believed with in our Virtuous Women's prayer group. The first one is written by our chairperson, Jeri Henry and the next two by Cheryl Thompson. Both of these women are dynamic women of God with a strong belief and faith in God, God's promises, and God's love.

A Miracle Shared by Jeri Henry
(in her words)

"The hardest thing about selecting a miracle to share is deciding on what to share. I have experienced so many miracles, and as I reflect on my life, I realize how blessed I have been. However, one of the miracles I treasure the most is the life of my youngest son.

"When I was three months pregnant, I started bleeding, and the doctors could not stop it. The bleeding continued for a month, and the doctors thought I was going to lose my baby. We prayed, and I called out to God to save my baby. That danger passed, and I was able to carry my child and enjoy my pregnancy. Everything went well until I was in my seventh month of pregnancy. My faith was challenged again when my doctor thought my baby might have a birth disorder. He wanted to run some tests that would have been dangerous for my unborn baby, but I said no. I trusted God to take care of my baby, and whatever happened, I knew God was in control. My husband, my prayer group, and I prayed that my baby would be a miracle. Today, I have a healthy, strong, smart, and handsome son. I know that God does hear prayers and He listens when his children cry out to him."

Two Miracles Shared by Cheryl Thompson
(in her words)

"I suffered from migraine headaches for several years. Sometimes, they were so severe I would become nauseated. I continued to pray and trust God's Word, and the Lord caused the headaches to gradually subside. I have been completely healed from that condition for approximately ten years. One of my healing Scriptures is Psalm 30:2: 'O Lord my God, I cried unto thee, and thou hast healed me.'

"In 2008, a tornado came through my neighborhood. I was at work, but during the storm, my family was in our basement and witnessed the powerful winds and flying debris. When I arrived at the entrance of our neighborhood, a large tree had fallen across the road. I had to drive through my neighbor's yard to get around it. However, God spared all of our homes and there was no serious damage, even though there are many trees.

"The next day, I noticed that all the trees in the front and back of my home were leaning in the same direction. The miracle is that God caused the wind to separate and go around my home, instead of going directly into it. I praise and trust God, and always trust in His promises, such as those of Psalm 91, for His divine protection."

A Miracle Shared by Sister Willie Mae Crump (in her words)

Sister Willie Mae Crump is a living miracle. She always amazes me that she is able to do so much, and as a senior citizen, she is so active. She is intelligent, spiritual, sensitive, compassionate, energetic, and able to do many things. She herself has written a book of poetry titled, *Rhymes for Reasons: A Personal Journey of Praise and Prayer*. Willie Mae didn't give me a miracle to report concerning herself, but gave me one concerning her brother, as follows:

"My brother has a history of heart disease. He experienced his first heart attack in November 1987 and has had two more since then. The last two required triple by-pass surgeries. During the last by-pass, my brother's doctor said that his heart was so damaged he was not certain of what might happen during and after the surgery. During the early morning hours in 2006, my mother received a call from my sister who was at the hospital with my brother. His doctor had just informed her to go ahead and call the funeral home that we planned to use because our brother would probably only last another few hours. My sister spoke with my mother and informed her of the situation. Although she knew who we wanted to use, she decided to get dressed and go to the hospital.

"We arrived an hour or so later and things really did look grim for my brother's life. But thanks be to God who is in control of everything, the doctor said, 'No, he will live.' And as of this very moment, he is still alive! Recently, he celebrated his eightieth birthday on April 25, 2015. What the doctor didn't know was that God and only God says when life is over. I am convinced the prayers that were prayed for my brother, John, were heard in heaven, and God spared his life.

"Just as a reminder, this is the same brother who was found lying in his bathtub unconscious in 2008. When the paramedics came, they checked his blood sugar and it was over 1200. His doctor verified the high level and stated that he has known people to have a blood sugar level that high, but they did not live.

"Over and over again, a number of his family members have said to him that the Lord is letting you live for a reason. It is incredible what this man has been through, but the Lord has shown him favor."

Author's Note: I thank Willie Mae for this astounding testimony. As you see, this is another incredible miracle. This gives more proof of God's infinite love and mercy and that life is in the hand of God. Not even skilled and trained doctors can predict the finality of life.

A Knee Miraculously Healed Shared by Gayle Harold

Recently at our church, God has been doing a new thing. He is manifesting the presence of the Holy Spirit in a very powerful way. One Wednesday in May after our usual Bible study, I overheard two of the regular members talking about their pains. I felt led to approach them and said, "Why don't we go into the chapel and pray?" I immediately asked Dr. Penn (John) to pray with us. The first person we prayed with was Gayle Harold, a young-looking grandmother.

In March, Gayle was having a hard time getting in and out of bed because of the tremendous pain in her knee. The pain was so great that she told the usher ministry she had been a part of that she would need to take a leave of absence. She even stopped going to Noonday Bible Study. She had only come that particular day because it was a new study for the summer and she needed to get the book so she could study at home. She had been trying to alleviate the pain by taking 800 mg. of Motrin, which began to give her nose bleeds. On one occasion, her nose bled for four hours, and she had to place a sponge in her nose the entire time.

James and Eleanor, regular attendees of the Noonday Bible Study, suggested that she have the Penns (John and I) to pray for her. But Gayle had heard another minister teach that you should pray for yourself, so she hesitated to ask us. She had been told by a doctor to have surgery, and it was also suggested that she have steroid injections. This she refused to do. Even though she continued to take the Motrin, she had so much pain that she couldn't sleep. Gayle also previously had therapy in September 2012, but still she was in pain.

That day, when John and I prayed for Gayle, she simply explained that she had a lot of pain in her knee. I placed my hand on her knee, and John prayed a simple, powerful prayer that God, in the name of Jesus, would heal her. After prayer, John asked her to do something she hadn't been able to do before. Gayle was immediately able to raise her leg without pain. We praised and rejoiced, thanking the Lord for what he was doing and had done in healing Gayle's knee. Now, several months later, she has informed her doctor that she has no more pain. She not only continues to have no pain, but she is able to go up and down the stairs like a teenager, and she also goes downstairs to her basement where her office is located. Previous to the Lord Jesus healing her, she had not gone to the basement because of her knee pain. Her husband, James, calls it a miracle, and we agree.

A Miracle Shared by Annette Moore

This year, our church has placed more focus on having a time for those who desire to come to the altar for prayer. During one of these times, Reverend Moore, our pastor, made a spontaneous decision. Sensing and discerning the presence of the Holy Spirit, he asked me to pray a prayer of healing. As he instructed, I led in prayer for those coming to the altar. Many of those present responded to the opportunity to come to the altar for healing prayer. Annette was one of those persons.

Annette is a trusted and faithful steward of our congregation. For four weeks she had been having stomach pains near or in the area of her intestines. She experienced this pain, especially as she drove over bumps in the road. During this altar prayer, she made the decision to come to the altar and seek the Lord's healing grace. She prayed this earnest prayer in faith: "In the name of Jesus, please heal this. I don't know what it is. Lord please heal this, restore and make it normal." As she prayed, something like a wind moved around the altar from the right to the left. She also felt something as she got up. Later, when she drove over the speed bump, the pain was no longer there.

Annette shared her healing four or five months later. She was still completely free of the pain she had experienced. Notice that Annette used the word *wind*, to express what moved near her as she prayed at the altar. In Scripture, *wind* refers to the Holy Spirit. Jesus, in talking to Nicodemus about being born again and how the Spirit gives birth to spirit, said: *"The wind blows wherever it pleases. You hear its sound, but you cannot tell where it comes from or where it is going. So it is with everyone born of the Spirit"* (John 3:8). Here we see that the Holy Spirit not only enables us to be "born again" in our spirits, but brings forth the healing power of God.

Miracle of Buying a Home—Joan Carter (in her words)

Joan is a member of the church we attend and a faithful servant of God. She has worked many years with our Sunday school, including serving as Sunday school superintendent. She also has a passion for the "least of these" and has reached out to them in special ways. About a year and a half ago, her husband, James Carter, also a faithful servant of God passed away. He served the church as trustee and Sunday school teacher for many years. Here Joan shares in her own words:

"My husband passed away about fifteen months ago. We had been married for forty-three years. His passing was traumatic for me. As a Christian woman, I do believe that my husband is with the Father and I will see him again. However, this past year has been very difficult.

"My husband and I used to frequently pass a green house not far from my present home. I always liked the house, but my husband said it was too small for us. One day, I passed the house and noticed that it was for sale. I had been praying and asking God what I should do about the big house I was in. I asked him to find me a house. I decided that God must be speaking to me and this was the house I was meant to have. So, nervously, I put my house up for sale. It sold in three days, and I made an offer on the green house. When it was inspected, many structural and plumbing issues were found that needed to be fixed before it would be habitable. I went back to God and asked Him what I should do. He told me this was not the house He had for me and I should terminate the contract. He told me He would find a house for me by noon that day. So, being obedient, I called my realtor and told her that I wanted to terminate the contract.

"I called my twin sister in California (I am in Georgia) and told her what had transpired. She said that God would work it out. In the meantime, I went on a Website here in Georgia to see if I could find a house. At the same time, my sister was on a different Website in California, looking for a house. She called me all excited and said, "I found you a house!" I said that I had found one, too. When she told me the address, it was the same house that I had found and was looking at right then! God is so awesome! That was a confirmation for me from God. It was after 12:00 noon in Georgia, but not in California.

"I called my realtor and said that I had to see that house. When I walked into it, I knew this was the house for me. My realtor even commented that the house felt like me. I moved into my new home in two weeks. God kept His promise, and I am truly blessed."

The Healing of Evangelist Marinda Turner
(in her words)

Following is an account of the healing of Evangelist Marinda Turner. She is a dynamic Christian with a deep faith in God and a strong belief in prayer. We became friends, and in response to my request, she agreed to share the following true story of her miraculous healing.

"In mid-October 1975, while I was employed as an English teacher at Alzheimer High School in the small town of Alzheimer, Arkansas, I became ill with congestive heart failure, pneumonia, and the flu, simultaneously. The trouble started on a Saturday afternoon. I had been feeling sick all morning, but I thought it would soon go away. My middle son happened to be at home that day. A friend of mine had called to see how I was doing. She advised me to go to the emergency room to have my condition checked.

"Suddenly, I began feeling tightness in the center of my chest. It seemed as if someone was taking a string and tightening a noose around my heart. Gasping for air, I asked my son to rush me to the hospital because I could not breathe. We jumped in the car, and he sped to Jefferson Hospital. When we got to the emergency room, they quickly rolled me down the hall and into a room where the nurses and doctors gave me shots and medicine. They inserted an IV, and suddenly I was able to breathe again.

"The next day, I was very ill, but I thought I would be feeling much better in a few days. I was in the hospital five or six days. When I was dismissed to go home, the doctor said my body was completely exhausted, and I needed much rest. Weeks of recuperating turned into months, and months into years.

"During the first six weeks, my husband took me from room to room like he would have carried a baby. I was just that weak. I could not sleep at night because my chest would hurt all night, each night. I would go to sleep around 5:00 a.m., and I would sleep until it was time to eat and take my medicine at 8:00 or 9:00 a.m. One of my cousins would come to clean my house and change the bed linens for no charge. She had once worked in my home on weekends.

"After a couple of months of so much pain, I called the doctor to tell him how badly I felt from the pain in my chest. He told me to cover my head and wait. There was nothing else he could do for me. At that very moment I turned to Almighty God and prayed this prayer:

"'Dear God, the doctor has given up on me, but I am sitting on your knee asking you to hold me, help me, and heal me, in the name of Jesus. I know I have been praying, but this time, I am turning my life over to you. I know you can heal my body, my mind, my spirit, and everything about me. I know you can because all power is in your hand. I am now waiting for you to intervene.

"'Oh God, my youngest son is only ten years old, and he needs me in his life because he is a rather difficult child to rear. Lord, I give it all to you. I will speak for you for the rest of my life. Lord, come to my rescue. Heal my body, in Jesus' name. Amen.'

"God began to heal me at that instant, although it was a very slow process. I waited patiently on the Lord. I went from the bed to the couch and from the couch to the bed for several years.

"At the time, my mother was living with us because she was unable to live alone. She set part of her kitchen on fire at her home. My husband taught high school mathematics and drove the school bus each day. Nevertheless, he would leave school and come home at lunch time to put two frozen dinners in the oven for me and my mother. I was unable to pick up a glass, so he bought paper goods, such as paper cups, plates and plastic flatware for us to use.

"After a year had passed, I began to feel better in the daytime although the nights were still a challenge. My mother was a self-taught seamstress, so during my second year of recuperation, I asked her to teach me to sew. She made garments without using a pattern; she could look at a garment and make one just like it. However, I bought patterns and fabric after learning how to use the sewing machine. By the third year of getting stronger, I began to make skirts, blouses, dresses, suits, and whatever I wanted to make. Gradually, I learned to sew quite well. Yet, I became concerned that I would never be able to return to work again. I truly loved teaching.

"After the third year of being unable to work, I asked the doctor how long he had a patient to stay disabled after a congestive heart failure. He said five years. At that moment I felt relieved, because that meant I had at least two more years to go before I needed to worry about returning to work. During the sixth year, I had enough strength to walk short distances. The doctor advised me to do only what I felt like doing and take my rest. I never forgot that advice; I use it to this day.

"In 1984, I returned to the classroom part time as a substitute teacher in the Pine Bluff School District. God had healed me completely. Oh, what an awesome God we serve! I was so happy to go back to work again. My life had come full circle. God had performed a miracle in my life.

In 1989, my former college teacher, who had retired, called to ask if I would accept an adjunct position as an English instructor at the University of Arkansas at Pine Bluff (UAPB) in her stead. I gladly accepted the offer and worked there for eleven years until I retired in 2003. In 2000, I answered God's call to the ministry. Even though I was too old for the itinerate ministry, I was so happy to receive my preaching license from the Elder, and I received my first appointment as an evangelist from the Bishop of the Twelfth Episcopal District. I received an appointment each year. I was so happy to live to fill many pulpits and do those things I promised God I would do. He allowed me to live long enough to do His will, and I am so thankful. In old age, my services have become more challenging, but God will always give me the strength and courage to do His will in my lifetime.

"God brought me from a bed-ridden patient to an active servant in His vineyard over a period of fifteen years. I am so grateful I have this opportunity to serve God and my fellow man. It is truly a blessing and God's favor on my life. This is my testimony of how God performed a miracle of healing and gave me the victory of a more abundant life. I am still on the battle field for the Lord."

Author's Note: This testimony truly demonstrates what God will do in our lives when we trust in Him. When the doctor had given up on Evangelist Turner's healing, she chose to turn to God and pray for God's healing grace. She could have believed the words of the doctor and made the choice to prepare to die. Instead, she chose to put her complete trust in God. Trusting in God is most important to experiencing God's miracles.

Gloria Moore (in her words)

The following miracle is an excellent illustration of how God causes all things to work together for good when we trust God and come to God for help. It is written in the words of the First Lady, Mrs. Gloria Moore of Allen Temple Methodist Church, where the Senior Pastor is Rev. Carl Moore, Sr. It encourages all parents to know that God looks beyond our faults and blesses us in spite of ourselves.

"The Lord saved my husband in July 1982, and I got saved in June 1983. My eyes were opened, and I began my walk with the Lord. My husband was called into ministry and was busy working a full time job, going to seminary, and serving as a minister of music at our church. One day I was walking on the track at the high school, the Lord spoke to me, saying, 'Go home and talk to your oldest daughter because she is pregnant.' I said this couldn't be true. I had been walking closely with the Lord, doing His work (I was youth director of our church), and paying tithes. How could this happen? I left the track and went home.

"Arriving at home, I found my daughter on the phone, while my husband was in his office studying. Right away, I asked her if she was pregnant. At first, her answer was no, but then she answered yes. I was devastated. I called my husband out of his office. My younger daughter had heard the conversation and came running out of her room, crying. My oldest daughter was a senior in high school and it was March. We prayed as a family and asked for God's guidance.

"We talked to the young man who was the father, and he stated that he loved our daughter and wanted to marry her when he was financially able. At that time, he was working in the Reserves. We discussed the need for a child to have both parents, and he agreed, but stated he would need help financially. We met with his parents and decided to have a wedding in celebration and not to hide. My husband made an announcement to the church during the 11 a.m. service and asked for the church to pray. It was a very emotional time.

"My daughter was very smart academically and had applied to several colleges. She had been accepted at all of them, but was offered a scholarship to Tuskegee University. To show how God works miracles, the young man had applied to only one college and had been accepted at—guess which one—Tuskegee. To further show how God was working, the young man's sister, who was already a student at Tuskegee, lived in a two-bedroom apartment and needed a roommate.

"The wedding was held in June, they went to Tuskegee in August, and the baby was born two days before semester break. My daughter received four As and one B; her husband passed all of his classes. We helped them financially, but because they were a family with very little income, they were eligible for all kinds of grants. They had a built in babysitter—his sister. My daughter and son-in-law had a good college experience, pledging a sorority and fraternity. During the summer before her senior year, my daughter was even able to go to New York to work on her master's degree. She graduated with the honor of Magna Cum Laude. Her husband graduated the next year. She worked in the

Tuskegee area as a teacher while he finished college. His sister graduated also."

Authors Note: The Lord used this pregnancy to show how what we considered an embarrassing situation to bring glory to God's name. Indeed, when we trust and believe in God, God can work all things *"for the good of those who love him"* (Rom. 8:28).

The Healing of Gwendolyn Jones
(in her words)

The following miracle was shared by Gwendolyn Jones, who was, in October 1986, a clinical supervisor at a large metropolitan VA medical center in Detroit, Michigan. One morning in November she discovered a small mass on the right side of her neck and immediately thought it was a swollen lymph node.

Although two of her co-workers encouraged her to see a doctor, it was awhile before she did so. Finally she made an appointment on December 19. The doctor recommended that she see a surgeon. While paying her bill, she scanned a list of names, Dr. Ander De Resto Soto's name jumped out at her, so she immediately called his office. Although it was the Friday before Christmas, his nurse scheduled her for an appointment. This worked out just fine because Dr. D's office was only two blocks from her church where she was planning a Christmas party for the children.

The next day, Saturday, she dropped the children off at the church and arrived at the doctor's office at 11:59 a.m. After a preliminary examination, Dr. D, who looked very much like Dr. Marcus Welby on television—with white hair, blue eyes, and small, speckled frame glasses— asked her what hospital she wanted to go to. Her response was that she wasn't going to go to a hospital. Dr. D placed both of her hands in his and explained that the mass on her neck needed to be removed. He explained that if she didn't have the mass removed immediately, the Christmas she planned to spend with her family might be her last. With those words from the surgeon, she agreed to go to the hospital the following Monday.

This news proved to be devastating; she doesn't even remember how she got back to the church. Gwen was hysterical and cried out to God. She was only thirty-nine years old. She immediately went to the altar, crying uncontrollably. The woman who was helping her with the Christmas party for the children said, "Baby, whatever it is, let's give it to God, so we can help these children enjoy their party." After they prayed, she did go and have fun with the children, but she also realized that this might be the last party she would attend with her own three children.

Later, that night, she told her husband, but he refused to allow her to have a pity party. The church choir was having its Christmas party. In spite of the way she felt about going, he encouraged her to go. Now to continue in her own words:

"He said that he was not going to participate in my pity party and I needed to be around strong Christian people who cared about me, so we were going to the party. We went. I shared my news and asked about thirty people to pray for me. They did, and then we had a party. When we went to church on Sunday, I went to the altar call. Everyone had prayed and left the altar, everyone but me. I don't know how long everyone else had been finished, but the pastor finally put both hands on my shoulders. I stood up and he asked me if I wanted to share what had me so burdened. When I told the congregation my situation, people knelt at their seats and the entire church prayed for me.

"Sunday night I dreamed it was thundering, lightning, and raining very hard. We always left the hall light on at night so the kids could see if they had to go to the bathroom during the night. In my dream, the hall light kept flickering.

From the hall, I heard a voice say not to worry about the outcome of the surgery, but I should know that the tumors would be cancerous, and I would be just fine. When the light stopped flickering, I woke up. I actually got up and went out into the hall. I didn't see anybody. After all, it was a dream, but it seemed so real. I went back to sleep and slept through the night."

After a wonderful Christmas dinner with her family, including her sister and her dad, Gwen went to the hospital the next morning at 6:00 a.m. Doctor D talked to her and explained that if the tumor was benign, she could go home after three days, but if it was malignant, she would have to go back to surgery for a thyroidectomy. To continue in Gwen's own words:

"When I woke up in the recovery room, Dr. D was at my bedside. He had tears in his eyes. I told him not to worry, that God had told me there were two malignant tumors, but I would be fine. He looked surprised. He said you're right, there were two tumors. He said I would be in extreme pain once the anesthesia wore off. He said that he had removed the tumor from the right side and sent down a section for examination. The pathologist called the OR to let them know the tumor was benign, so he sutured me up, applied a dressing over the site, and removed the intubation tube. I was being transferred to the recovery room when the pathologist met the nurses transporting me to say they needed to take me back to the OR. After further review, he had determined the tumor was malignant. The doctor also said that it had taken him much longer for the second surgery because they found a second tumor on the left side. He was really surprised that the tumor hadn't spread, and both tumors were primary."

After seeing Gwen on Monday morning, Dr. D called her a walking miracle. He had never seen someone heal so quickly, particularly from the type of surgery she had gone through. Gwen told him that he was an excellent surgeon, but God, the Ultimate Healer, had been in control in that operating room and Dr. D had just followed His lead. God had directed his hands. He said, 'Mrs. Jones, I believe what you say is true."

Gwen healed quickly and went back to work in March 1987. She has been cancer free for almost twenty-eight years. She says, "To God be the glory! By Jesus' stripes I was healed. You can't tell me God is not a Healer. You can't tell me what God can't do. I know He can and will. He did it for me, and He keeps doing it over and over again. He'll do it for you too." Gwen says that the experience gives her an opportunity to witness for God and encourages others in similar situations. The experience has made her a better nurse, and she thanks God for using her. This indeed is a great example of how God works through doctors to bring about his great miracles.

The above miracles are all accounts revealing the faithfulness and love of a Living God who is present and available to us all. God's works, in Christ are manifested in many marvelous ways.

Six

God Works Miracles in Mysterious Ways

Some years before John became an ordained minister, he was a part of the lay mission in the area where we lived in Delaware. On one of the lay mission trips, John and his fellow workers in Christ went to Philadelphia to share their testimonies with a church congregation. During the testimony, John shared about being delivered from drinking alcohol shortly after receiving salvation. John was never an alcoholic; he did drink on the weekends, but not to excess. Still, John knew that God had done something miraculous in him because he now had no desire whatsoever to drink socially or otherwise. After the men shared their testimonies, one of the ladies present in the congregation came to John and asked him to pray for her husband who truly was an alcoholic. But before they could pray for her husband, the lady was given the news that her son "Chip" was extremely ill at home; he had just had an asthma attack. The group of men gathered in a circle around Chip's mother, and as John led in prayer, they prayed that God would heal Chip and free him from asthma. While they prayed, the awesome presence of the Holy Spirit was experienced by all present. John describes it as a glorious anointing of God's love. They felt that Jesus' healing presence was there to heal.

Some weeks later, John was told that Chip was completely healed. Not only was he healed, but his father, having witnessed the miracle of his son being healed of asthma, was immediately delivered from drinking alcohol. In this testimony, we may note that neither Chip nor his father was present during the time of prayer. Still, both were miraculously healed, one physically and the other both spiritually and physically. This manifestation of healing reminds me of the prayer request made of Jesus by the centurion.

The Gospel of Matthew reveals that when Jesus entered Capernaum, a centurion came to him and asked him for help with a servant who was at home paralyzed and in "terrible suffering" (Matt. 8:8-10). Jesus proceeded immediately to go to heal him, but the centurion responded:

> Lord, I do not deserve to have you come under my roof, But just say the word, and my servant will be healed. For I myself am a man under authority, with soldiers under me. I tell this one, 'Go,' and he goes; and that one 'Come,' and he comes. I say to my servant, 'Do this,' and he does it." Jesus was astonished at these words and said to those with him, 'I tell you the truth, I have not found anyone in Israel with such great faith.'

Here we see not only the faith of the centurion, but that the power and the authority of Jesus Christ are not limited by time or space. We can pray for a person in one place and God will heal him miles away. God does truly work in mysterious ways, God's miracles to perform.

Miracles of God's Intervention in Unexpected Ways

Sometimes, the Lord will surprise us and answer our prayers in the most unexpected ways. God may intervene in our lives when we least expect it. One such instance occurred in our lives when we took an anniversary/vacation trip to Montreal, Canada. We had not planned our trip months before hand as some do, but decided to begin planning about a month before the date to leave. We called our sister-in-law, Jeanette, who worked with a travel agency, to ask for her assistance. She helped us, through use of our computers, from where she lived in Lawrenceville, Georgia. We wanted a non-stop flight from Philadelphia to Montreal. At the time, we lived in Middletown, Delaware, and the airport in Philadelphia was the closest to us. It seemed that all was going well. After some time, we found the flight we wanted and proceeded to put in our credit card account number, but for some reason, the computer would not accept the number. We tried everything we could think of to correct the problem. Finally, we reluctantly decided to use another credit card, but when we got back to the computer, the non-stop flight for the price we wanted was no longer available. It was quite a disappointment. Even Jeanette was not able to help us.

The day came for us to start our trip. We were not looking forward to changing planes in some out of the way city and taking hours longer than we planned to reach our destination. When we got to the airport, to our amazement and great surprise, we found out that our flight had been canceled and we had been placed on a non-stop flight. Hallelujah, the Lord does give us our heart's desires!

Later, as if something was trying to place a damper on our God-given blessing, we arrived in Canada, only to discover that our suitcases were not there. We waited for over an hour, going from place to place, trying to locate our luggage, and waiting to talk to someone who might help us.

Still not knowing where our bags were or when we would get them, we got into our rental car and headed for the hotel. Our anniversary was the next day, and we were looking forward to dressing up and going out for a delicious fish dinner. The next day, as we prepared to go to dinner, we called the airport, and still our suitcases had not been located. We got over our disappointment, deciding we would not allow this situation to ruin our anniversary, by being upset. We would just take our showers, put on our same clothes, and still have a good time. An hour before we were ready to leave, there was a knock at the door. There, when we least expected it, were our bags. You can imagine how John and I rejoiced. We quickly changed our clothes and proceeded on to dinner.

Another surprise that God blessed us with during this time was a refrigerator in our room. We had been told we would have to pay an extra twenty-five dollars a day to have a refrigerator in our room. Much to our surprise, we did have a refrigerator in our room at no additional charge. God is good!

God loves us and wants us to be happy and at peace. God only desires the best for us. When we are consistent in our trust and faith in God, we reap a harvest of God's love and blessings. Whether the blessings are small or large, they are testaments to a faithful and caring God who is always there for us. *The important thing is that when we pray, we not pray our fears, but pray the victory that we desire in our lives.* If we abide in Christ, as the Scripture points out, and his words abide in us, we cannot fail. Remember, the victory is to those who faithfully abide in Christ, for Christ abides in the Father, and we, as Christians, abide in Christ (John 15:7).

God Gives Us Our Hearts' Desire
(John's trip to see the Inauguration)

For some time, John had been in prayer about attending the inauguration, but he didn't feel that he had the funds to go. One morning, he woke up with a feeling of being compelled to go. It seemed impossible, because now it was Monday morning, just one day before President Obama's inauguration. When John told me he was going to Washington, D.C., I was truly perplexed at such a late decision and wondered how he would be able to arrange to go in such a short period of time. There were obstacles not only concerning the time element, but the cost to go at such a late date. This did not deter John. He called the airport to see if flights were available. A flight was available, surprisingly, at a good rate. In fact, they had a special. He then called his Hilton Honors account and, believe it or not, a hotel room close to D.C. was available. Not only was a room available where John had on one occasion stayed, but it was available at the regular rate. John packed very quickly and was able to contact our son, Stephen, to take him to the airport, even though he had to travel from his home in Atlanta.

After John's arrival at the airport in Baltimore, he checked into the hotel and discovered that a group of people staying at the hotel were also going to the inauguration. They had hired a school charter bus to take them to the inauguration and pick them up and return them to the hotel. Guess what? There was only one seat left. Finding the person in charge, he immediately made a reservation and purchased a ticket. This was indeed a great relief since John had anticipated a lot of transportation changes in getting to D.C.

They left at six o'clock the next morning on their way to D.C. When they arrived in D.C., the group discovered they each needed a ticket to get on the mall. They did not become discouraged, but continued to the mall. Amazingly, a few tickets were still left. God, as in all the other necessities for the trip, had also worked this out, opening every door and blessing John to be at this historic event. The only concern was the extreme cold. He did not realize how cold and stiff his legs would be from standing in the cold for the inauguration, but once he arrived home, as he continued to walk, his legs began to feel better. For several days, he felt discomfort in his legs, but months later, there was no sign of stiffness. What an amazing miracle!

The power of God is not limited, controlled, or dependent on what we have. God is awesome. If we are willing to believe and if we are willing to step out in faith, God can make a way out of no way.

A Miracle of Persistent Faith

The next miracle is a modern-day story of God's intervention and an example of persistence in prayer. I would like to begin with a parable lesson, given by Jesus.

In this parable, Jesus gives an account of a persistent widow who courageously comes before a judge of power and position. Even though he is quite a formidable person, she does not let fear come into her heart and stop her from being persistent in asking for justice.

Even when the judge refuses her request, she continues to come before the judge. She continues to keep on knocking, for the Scripture says, *"For some time he [the judge] refused"* (Luke 18: 4a) In spite of the fact that he does not fear God or man, he eventually gives in to this widow so that, as he said, he would not be worn out by her (constant) coming (vv. 4b-5). The Scripture clearly points out that if this unjust judge would do what he did, surely God will bring about justice for those who are God's children. For those who cry out to him day and night, for those who persist and do not give up, God will make sure they receive justice and they will receive it quickly!

What God wants us to realize is that perseverance in prayer is an important part of being a person of faith. Jesus says at the end of the parable, *"However, when the Son of Man comes, will he find faith on the earth?"* (Luke 18:8b).

This parable relates to the Scripture that tells us we have not, because we ask not. We also have the Scripture that tells us to *"Ask and it will be given to you; seek and you will find; knock and the door will be opened to you. For everyone who asks will receive, [those] who seek will find, and for [those] who knock, the door will be opened"* (Matt. 7:7-8). Here, we also see the admonition of persistent prayer. For, if we look at the meaning of the language background of how this is written in Greek, these words indicate that we should keep on asking, keep on seeking, keep on knocking, or we should constantly ask, we should constantly seek, and we should constantly knock. To say it in yet another way, we should persistently ask, persistently seek, and persistently knock.

Here is an amazing personal example. It all began when my father passed away in 2007. He had requested that he be buried beside my mother. Now this appears to be a very simple request, but since the time Mother passed and was buried in December 1977, several other persons had been buried around my mother. It was apparent that my father could not be buried there, so it was determined that my father be buried about sixty feet or more away on the other side of the cemetery.

I just did not have any peace about this. I asked about the possibility of later on having my mother's vault exhumed and placed beside my father at a later date. Mr. Sadler, who was in charge of the burial operations, said yes, it could be done. When I asked about the cost, he replied that it would cost about $2,000. My cousin said, "It really doesn't matter;

it's just a body." True, but I still was not at peace. I went back to the area where my mother was buried and began to intensely (fervently) try to find a space. As I did this, it was apparent that there were head stones, two to three feet beyond my mother's grave and also, two to three feet behind. It appeared there was no way that any space could be available, but still I had no peace. I mentioned my concern to John and he said they should be able to push something like a rod into the ground to determine if there was a space next to my mother. My cousin, Mary, said she knew that they did have what is called a probe to determine if someone is buried in a certain area.

By this time Mr. Sadler was on the tractor, the vault was attached to the chain hanging from the tractor, and it was being taken to the area where it would be buried. As he drove in the opposite direction from my mother's grave, I said to my husband, "Ask Mr. Sadler if he can probe the ground to see if there is any available space." "Hurry," I added.

John ran toward the tractor. I had no idea Mr. Sadler had a probe with him. He stopped the tractor and immediately came over with his probe. Mr. Sadler could have told me there was no way that there could be a space. On top of that, everyone else was looking at me like I was crazy. But I continued to pray and I continued to persevere. I kept on knocking.

Mr. Sadler took the probe and each time he pushed it into the ground, he was more and more convinced that nobody was buried in that small area. He said the only possibility was that a person was buried there many years ago, who had not been placed in a vault. My brother looked at me and said, "Give it up." Then something just rose up in me, and I said, "I'm not giving it up." With that, I walked away.

But, I came back. I called my brother over and said, "Come and listen to what the experts, Mr. Sadler and his helper are saying." Their words were most encouraging. They felt that because the probe was taking quite a bit of strength to push into the ground, the dirt in this small area had never been removed. Also, as they continued to probe, the probe did not seem to hit anything. From their experience, if the ground was hard (the probe was difficult to push into the ground), the dirt had not been removed; if the ground was soft (the probe easily went into the ground), the dirt had been removed and there was probably someone buried there. Once, the dirt is removed, it never goes back to the way it originally was.

After testing the ground, they went to get the tractor. This was quite a job because the area where they had planned to bury my father was full of moisture (it had been raining) and the tractor kept getting stuck. John, seeing the situation, suggested that Mr. Sadler move the tractor a certain way. (I wondered how he knew, but it seems that God was giving him wisdom.) Now, all of this time, I had been praying—praying for a space near my mother, praying they could get the tractor moving, praying God would help and give wisdom to those who were doing the work. (In other words, I kept on knocking). Finally, the tractor was back to more solid ground and moved over to the area next to my mother. They began to dig out the dirt with the tractor. They had to dig down at least four feet to be sure that there was not a body in the area. Each time the backhoe went down I prayed that they would not strike anything. Finally, the Lord told me that I was not to worry about it. He had it all planned and everything was going to be alright. Now, I wasn't one hundred percent sure I was hearing from God, but I was about to find out.

I, along with everyone present, watched intently each time the backhoe went down into the ground. About ten minutes later, the burial site was all cleared out and amazingly, the backhoe never touched anything. My father's vault was lowered as if it were always meant to be there. All was well. At that moment, I experienced a peace that was glorious and full of joy. I went to those who had been looking at me so strangely and said, "See what God can do?" They had to acknowledge that God had done an amazing thing.

What I experienced was truly the work of the Lord, but if I had given up and just let it be, I never would have experienced the fruits of persistent/persevering prayer and action. I have to give credit to my husband who supported me in my actions and prayers, and also did not give up. The Scripture says, *"if two of you on earth agree about anything you ask for, it will be done for you by my Father in heaven"* (Matt. 18:19). Mr. Sadler said that burying my father there actually saved us half of the cost. I also realized this was a much better place, for where they were going to originally place my father was full of moisture and they would have had to wait until the area dried out. The area where my mother was buried was on higher ground, and when it rained, the water ran down to the area where they were going to place my father.

At times, God requires persistent prayer, persevering prayer, and prayers that work together in action and faith. For *"without faith it is impossible to please God"* (Heb. 11:6). Persevering prayer requires that we do not focus on circumstances; rather, we focus on God—God's promises, God's love, God's compassion. It is also of utmost importance that we be obedient when God has instructed us to do a certain thing. It is important that we give it all we've got. It is important that we persevere in prayer and action about the things that God desires for us to do and move forward according to what God has shown us or the vision God has given us. As we do this, as we persist and persevere in prayer, we will see many unusual manifestations and signs of God's love and glory. In God's heart is a special place for those who call on God's name with sincerity and persistence. We can bring forth fruit that will last, give God the glory, and be a great testimony of God's enduring love, power, and grace that come from the persevering prayers of God's servants, in the name of Jesus and in the power of the Holy Spirit. We've got to keep on knocking if we want to see God's miracles of life, of hope, and of love. This is truly a modern-day miracle of God's intervention.

A Miracle of Protection

Years ago, while we were living in Tulsa, I started having nightmares of something chasing me continuously, night after night. I asked the Lord what I could do about this. Immediately after my prayer, the thought came to me to read the 91st Psalm. As I read the psalm, I began to realize more and more that I could trust in God to protect me, no matter what situation I was in, even while asleep. The Psalm reads, *"He who dwells in the shelter of the Most High will rest in the shadow of the Almighty. I will say of the Lord, 'He is my refuge and my fortress, my God, in whom I trust'"* (vv. 1, 2). I realized that while I was asleep, the Lord was my refuge and fortress; indeed I could trust him to watch over me and protect me. At a later time, verses three and four became a *rhema* word for me, as well as a promise of Scripture. There were times when I would think of the possibility of breast cancer. This was natural, I suppose, because so many around me were having this health concern. But then I thought about the words, *"Surely he will save you from the fowler's snare and from the deadly pestilence. He will cover you with his feathers, and under his wings you will find refuge; his faithfulness will be your shield and rampart"* (vv. 3-4). These words gave me assurance that if I trusted in the Words of God, he would even protect me from the pestilence and disease, and that God is indeed faithful to God's Word.

Then verse five: *"You will not fear the terror by night, nor the arrow that flies by day, nor the pestilence that stalks in the darkness, nor the plague that destroys at midday."* This promise gave me more assurance that I need not fear what may be prowling around in the dark or what pestilence is lurking in the night or the day, for God, in Christ Jesus, is my protector. No matter what is happening around me, God will protect me.

The Scripture continues in verses 7 and 8: *"A thousand may fall at your side, ten thousand at your right hand, but it will not come near you. You will only observe with your eyes and see the punishment of the wicked."* I want to make it clear that I do not think those who develop a disease such as breast cancer love the Lord any less than I do. And, I know that God loves them just as much as God loves me, but I chose to believe these promises. God has been and still is faithful. Because they love and trust the Lord, even for those who develop a health concern, God will still deliver them, heal them, and make them whole.

The words of promise and assurance continue: *"If you make the Most High your dwelling—even the Lord, who is my refuge—then no harm will befall you, no disaster will come near your tent. For he will command his angels concerning you to guard you in all your ways, they will lift you up in their hands so that you will not strike your foot against a stone"* (vv. 9-12). These words and the remaining words of the 91st Psalm have never failed to give me the assurance that the Lord is with me and will protect me from any concern or spiritual attack that may try to invade my life. I believe this psalm has not only encouraged me toward the miraculous events in my life, but has encouraged many others.

II. THE EVIDENCE OF THINGS UNSEEN

Seven

The Miracle of the Holy Spirit

The Holy Spirit is a gift of power. It is a gift of authority and a gift of truth. The Holy Spirit is a gift given to us, as disciples of Christ, to lead us, guide us, and teach us all truth. The Spirit is a personal gift from Christ, who before he left this earth, according to the Gospel of John, told his disciples that he would not leave them alone, but he was sending the Paraclete, an advocate or comforter, to be with them. The Holy Spirit is the third person of the Trinity, who has always existed with God from the beginning, at the time of Christ Jesus, and now at the present time. The Spirit was and is sent to all who will receive Christ; in fact, the Holy Spirit represents the living presence of God.

In the Old Testament Scriptures, the Holy Spirit was a part of the creative process of life. It was the Spirit of the Lord who moved upon the waters as the earth was created. In the Book of Numbers, after Moses complained to God that he could not care for the people by himself (11:14), the Lord responded by instructing him to select seventy elders to come before him at the Tent of Meeting. When this was accomplished, God came in a cloud, spoke to Moses, then took some of the Spirit that was upon Moses and placed it on the seventy elders so they would be able to help Moses care for the people. When the Spirit came upon the seventy elders, they prophesied (11:25). Now, two elders, Eldad and Medad, remained in the camp, although they were listed with the other elders. The Spirit came upon them and they also prophesied (11:26-27).

The Spirit was also poured out upon the judges and the prophets of Israel. (In the beginning of their history as a nation, the people of Israel did not have kings to lead them; they had judges.) This we can see in the life of Samuel, who was both a judge and a prophet. Samuel, in obedience to God, anointed Saul as king, and as he prophesied to Saul, the Spirit of the Lord possessed Saul. When Saul met a band of prophets who were in a prophetic frenzy, he also went into a prophetic frenzy. Later, when Saul was rejected by the Lord as king because of his disobedience, Samuel was sent by God to anoint David as king, and *"from that day on the Spirit of the Lord came upon David in power"* (1 Sam. 16:13). Here we see that in David's situation, the Spirit was not given to him temporarily, but it was to be with him permanently. The prophets, Ezekiel, Elijah, Elisha and Isaiah, spoke of the Spirit in reference to themselves.

In the Old Testament Scriptures, the Spirit was only given to certain people and, to some of the people, only at certain times. But God had promised through the prophet Joel that a time would come when the Spirit would be poured out on all flesh. Joel 2:28-29 reads: *"I will pour out my Spirit on all people. Your sons and daughters will prophesy, your old men will dream dreams, your young men will see visions. Even on my servants, both men and women, I will pour out my Spirit in those days."*

It was through the life of Christ that this prophecy began to be fulfilled. In chapter three of Luke, the scene opens with John the Baptist preparing the way of the Lord. John declared, as he baptized his disciples, that he baptized with water *"for repentance. But after me will come one who is more powerful that I, whose sandals I am not fit to carry. He will baptize you with the Holy Spirit and with fire"* (Matt. 3:11). Later, as John baptized the one he was speaking of, who is Jesus, *"the Holy Spirit descended upon him in bodily form, like a dove. And a voice came from heaven, 'You are my Son, the Beloved; with you I am well pleased'"* (Luke 3:22 NRSV).

In Luke 4:14, Jesus returns to Galilee to begin his ministry and later to Nazareth. While in the temple, the scroll of the prophet Isaiah is given to him. He unrolls it and, from the writings of Isaiah, reads: *"The Spirit of the Lord is upon me, because he has anointed me to bring good news to the poor. He has sent me to proclaim release to the captives and recovery of sight, to let the oppressed go free, to proclaim the year of the Lord's favor"* (Luke 4:18-19 NRSV).

These are just illustrations of the work of the Holy Spirit in the life of humankind. In the gospel of John (20:19-22), we see that after the resurrection, Jesus appeared to the disciples and appointed them to go forth. He then breathed on them and told them to receive the Holy Spirit. For forty days, Jesus continued to show them that he was alive and to speak to them of the kingdom of God. Just before Jesus ascended into heaven, he told the disciples to remain in Jerusalem and wait for the Holy Spirit, the promise of the Father. They would receive power when the Holy Spirit would come upon them and they would be his witnesses *"in Jerusalem, and in all Judea and Samaria, and to the ends of the earth"* (Acts 1:8).

The Holy Spirit came, as Jesus had promised, at the time of Pentecost. It was during the time that the disciples had been gathering together in the Upper Room. It reads in Acts: *"They all joined together constantly in prayer, along with the women and Mary the mother of Jesus, and with his brothers"* (Acts: 1:18). The disciples had been daily waiting for the great promise. They had been devoting themselves to prayer, fellowship, and the study of the Word of God. Now that day had come, the time for the great promise to be fulfilled. It was the day of Pentecost, the day when they were all together. The disciples, about one hundred and twenty people, had been gathering in the Upper Room, praying and singing hymns of joy and praise to God.

As they are doing this, suddenly, from heaven there comes a violent and strong wind; and as it comes in, it fills the whole place where they are sitting. What an awesome sight, to see and know the presence of God in the coming of a mighty wind! Then most amazingly, they see tongues as of fire rest on each of them. To talk about it now seems almost unbelievable. *But, if God made the heavens and the earth, it is nothing for God to cause tongues of fire to settle on each person and not even cause a burn or a singe.* Then all of them—not some of them, all of them—are filled with the Holy Spirit and begin to speak in other languages as the Spirit gives them the ability (Acts 2:1-4).

This is the great promise of Jesus Christ, now fulfilled. As I explained earlier, Jesus had told the disciples he would send the Holy Spirit upon them, but the Spirit doesn't just come; it manifests itself in a powerful way. The Spirit comes in a mighty way, with a mighty message and a mighty plan. You see, this is not just any day. On this day of Pentecost, the people of Israel, the Jewish people, have come together to celebrate what is also called the Feast of Weeks, which occurs fifty days after Passover. People from many nations have gathered together to celebrate the goodness and faithfulness of God (*New Interpreter's Bible*, Acts, p. 53). They are amazed and astonished. Here are disciples who are Galileans, speaking each and every language of those represented in the crowd—not just one language, but several

The Miracle of the Holy Spirit

different languages. It reminds us of what took place at the tower of Babel (Gen. 11:1-9). There, God caused people to speak in different languages in order to confuse them, and they had no understanding of what the other was saying. But, now, they are united by the Spirit, speaking many different native languages, declaring the wonders of God. They are speaking of the power of God. Some are amazed and perplexed; others sneer and accuse them of being filled with new wine (Acts 2:5-12).

So here begins the birth of the Christian Church, and the Christian Church is alive with the presence of the Holy Spirit. Upon hearing this, amazingly, Peter stands up. This Peter, who three times denied Jesus out of fear, this Peter who had quietly been "laying low," this Peter now speaks with boldness of the Lord, Jesus Christ. Peter stands in the midst of the people, but he doesn't stand alone; the eleven other apostles stand with him. Peter raises his voice and exclaims: *"Men of Judea and all who live in Jerusalem let this be known to you, and listen to what I say. Indeed, these are not drunk, as you suppose, for it is only nine o'clock in the morning. No this is what was spoken through the prophet Joel"* (Acts 2:14b-16 NRSV).

Some people think of the Spirit as a nebulous, eerie, mysterious presence that only certain people can discern. But the Spirit is a person of power and authority. *The Spirit doesn't just come to make us feel good and make everything mysterious. The Spirit comes to transform us, to bring change. The Spirit comes to magnify God; the Spirit comes to speak the truth of Christ.* The Spirit comes to comfort us, lead us, and guide us in paths of righteousness and love. The Spirit can come gently when you least expect, but here we see the Spirit coming in majestic power and might. And at Pentecost, the Spirit comes with such terrific might and power that the

Scripture says the sound, the very sound brings a multitude of people together. The Spirit demands their attention.

Peter let them know in no uncertain terms that the Jesus who performed miracles, the Jesus who was delivered up to die on the cross, the one called Lord by David was this Jesus. He let them know that the Jesus who was raised up again by God was now at the right hand of the Father, who had promised the Holy Spirit, and what they are now seeing and hearing is Jesus pouring out upon them the promise of the Holy Spirit (Acts 2:22-33). Now the Spirit is taking this small group of women and men and bringing about a change in their hearts and minds. The Spirit, as Jesus had promised, is empowering them to be his witnesses.

What a difference a day makes. What a difference in twenty-four little hours. What a difference from one sunrise to the next sunrise. No longer are the disciples (apostles) hiding behind closed doors. Now they are boldly being seen by thousands of men and women as they proclaim the Word of God. What Jesus had promised is now being fulfilled. He told them they would be baptized in the Holy Spirit. He told them they would receive power when the Holy Spirit came upon them. He told them they would be his witnesses in Jerusalem, in Judea, in Samaria and *"even to the remotest part of the earth"* (Acts 1:8 NASB). No longer are they walking in fear and anxiety. Now they were walking boldly in the Spirit.

The "new Peter," now filled with Holy Spirit boldness, tells the people to repent and be baptized in the name of Jesus Christ for the forgiveness of their sins, and they will receive the gift of the Holy Spirit, for as he had just quoted from Joel, the promise is for them, their children, and *"for all whom the Lord our God will call"* (Acts 2:39). Here we see that the Spirit convicts those present of sin, tells of the righteousness of Christ, and brings judgment upon the evil forces that sought to condemn Christ. The Spirit has enabled those who are present to receive the message preached by Peter. And do you know what happens that day? Three thousand souls are added to the Church of God. Not just one, not just two, but three thousand persons receive Christ as their Lord and Savior.

Now they are filled with the living water that Jesus spoke to the Samaritan woman about in John 4. Yes, they are filled with rivers of living, refreshing, renewing waters. *They were now able to worship the Lord in Spirit and in Truth.* What a difference a day makes when the power of God is present by the Spirit. The disciples worship God in spirit and in truth, and those who are sick in their presence are miraculously healed. Yes, they manifest the power of the Holy Spirit, the Spirit of authority, and the Spirit of truth.

Before his ascension into heaven, and even before the resurrection, Jesus said he was not going to leave his disciples alone. He was sending the Holy Spirit to be our guide, to be our advocate, and to enable us to be powerful witnesses. So what is this Holy Spirit all about? God's Holy Spirit, who was with God from the beginning, gives us power to love, power to be God's witnesses, and power to speak God's Word with boldness. God's Spirit gives us power to understand God's Word, power in prayer, and power to use the gifts that each one of us as Christians has been given through our salvation. God's Spirit gives us power to live our Christian lives according to God's plan and will. God's Spirit teaches us and guides us into all truth.

Yes, God gives us power through the Holy Spirit to perform miracles. God gives ordinary people the power to do extraordinary things. Indeed, God uses the foolish things of the world to confound the wise and those who are weak to confound the strong (1 Cor. 1:27). Two biblical illustrations of this are Peter and Paul. We know how Peter denied knowing Christ even though he personally knew and loved the Lord. Not only Peter, but all of the disciples were in fear, though Peter did follow at a distance (Matt. 26:58). The other disciples ran for their lives as Jesus was brought before the high priest (Mark. 14:50). But we know that once Peter is filled with the Holy Spirit on the Day of Pentecost, he becomes a powerful teacher and preacher of the living God and he is no longer fearful of those who want to harm him. In fact, Peter is so filled with the Spirit that God performs through Peter one of the greatest miracles of the early church.

The miracle occurs as Peter and John are about to enter the temple gate called Beautiful at three in the afternoon for a time of prayer. A man crippled from birth had been placed by the gate, and when he sees Peter and John, he asks them for money. Peter says, *"'Look at us!' So the man gave them his attention, expecting to get something from them."* Then Peter says, *'Silver or gold I do not have, but what I have I give you. In the name of Jesus Christ of Nazareth, walk'"* (Acts 3:1-6). Peter then takes the lame man by his hand and raises him to his feet. As he does so, the man's feet and ankles instantly become strong. He is able to stand, and he begins walking, leaping and praising God (vv. 7-8).

As a result of this miracle, five thousand persons are added to the Church. God is doing extraordinary things through Peter in the power of the Holy Spirit. Here is an ordinary man being used by God in extraordinary ways. Here is evangelism at its best. God uses miraculous works to bring others to knowledge of salvation through Jesus Christ. My husband, John, often says, "The gifts of the Spirit are the evangelistic tools of the Church." Truly they are.

The Scripture tells us that after Paul is filled with the Holy Spirit, the power of the Spirit is so manifested in Paul's life that, even as he is being criticized by others, he becomes more and more powerful in his preaching and in manifesting the gifts of the Holy Spirit. God performs *"extraordinary miracles through Paul, so that even handkerchiefs and aprons that had touched him were taken to the sick and their illnesses were cured and the evil spirits left them"* (Acts 19:11-12).

Paul risks his life time after time to preach the gospel of Christ. He is so powerful in his preaching that many Jews seek to kill him. The Scripture tells us that Paul, himself, proclaimed that he was caught up to the third heaven. Once he comes to know Christ, Paul's amazing life would put the TV show, *Survivor*, to shame. Paul is the utmost survivor. Five times he survives receiving thirty-nine lashes, and his other sufferings include being beaten with rods three times, being stoned, and being shipwrecked three times. He is constantly in danger *"from rivers, in danger from bandits, in danger from my own countrymen, in danger from Gentiles, in danger in the city, in danger in the country, in danger at sea; and in danger from false brothers"* (2 Cor. 11:24-26). He goes without food and water and is cold and naked (v. 27); yet he continues to be an extraordinary survivor, teaching and preaching the Word of God in city after city. We know that in Damascus, the gates were guarded to make sure they would see him and kill him, but in the extraordinary move of God, the disciples let him down in a basket from a window in the wall and he escapes their hands (Acts 9:23-25). Truly Paul finds his strength and perseverance through the Lord. God has taken an ordinary man and performed extraordinary, miraculous things in his life. We too can do extraordinary, miraculous things in the power of the Holy Spirit. We too can be instruments of God's miraculous power!

Eight

From East to West—A Miracle That Takes Its Own Time

Earlier, I wrote of how the Lord spoke to John and told him that he would go from "East to West" to take God's healing power to his people. We rejoiced that God had spoken to John so powerfully. Sometime later, we were invited to several local churches to teach and pray with others. When God first spoke to John, we had three children, John II, Myrtle, and Jacqueline. Later, with three additional children, Mark, Christina, and Stephen (two of them still babies), we went to Tulsa. But John was not going from "East to West." John majored in theology, and three years later, received a degree in theology. We saw many miracles and ministered where God opened the doors. Still, John was not going from "East to West." Later, John became an ordained minister and pastor in the United Methodist Church, but still he was not going from "East to West."

During this time of ministry as a pastor, John spoke to everyone who would listen to him about God's healing grace. As an assistant pastor in a cross-racial appointment, the senior pastor told him he would never have teaching

From East to West—A Miracle That Takes Its Own Time

about healing in his church. John was quite disappointed in the pastor's rejection of the healing ministry. As a result, he found a new way to reach others with God's healing grace. He felt if he couldn't teach about healing in the church, he would write a booklet on healing. Most of the pastors he shared with concerning his calling to the healing ministry rejected this ministry. One pastor told him, "Get a church and settle down." Even after John completed his first booklet, *What Everyone Should Know About Healing*, and sent over fifty copies to other pastors, only one pastor in this area was encouraging.

Because of the rejection of his ministry and not seeing the things God had spoken to him fully come to pass, John could have become very discouraged. He had done all he could to prepare himself. He had earned degrees in Theology and Divinity, he had gone through the process of being ordained, had written a healing booklet, and still he was not going "East to West."

But God had a plan. In 1989, John met a dynamic director at the Upper Room, Dr. Jim Wagner, who was teaching at a conference in Baltimore. After the teaching session, John shared with him a copy of his booklet. Dr. Wagner really liked the booklet and said it was very much needed in his ministry. He informed John that for a long time, he had been looking for that kind of booklet to give to those he taught. A friendship developed between the two. Later, he asked John to teach with him on at least two occasions. Wherever he went, he always recommended John's booklet on healing. It is amazing that a booklet rejected by other ministers in the same denomination was now accepted by the Director of Spiritual Formation and Healing of the same denomination. In 1992, Jim Wagner decided to resign as director of this program of the Upper Room of the General Board of Discipleship and told John his plans. About this time, I started to pray intensely, on a daily basis, concerning God's guidance for John.

The first two years, after completing his degree in theology, John went back into teaching in the public schools. Then surprisingly, because of Jim Wagner's recommendation, he was asked to teach at the Bible and Evangelism Conference in Lake Junaluska. John did this for one week for several summers. We did not realize it then, but God was setting the stage.

John fasted and prayed concerning whether or not he should leave the United Methodist Church. God told him not to leave the church for there were doors that God was going to open that he would not have to open. Shortly after that, we visited Dr. Horner, who was a professor at Regent University and lived in Virginia Beach. When we visited Dr. Horner and his family, he had a distinguished guest, Dr. Ezekiel Guti, from Harare, Zimbabwe in Africa. Dr. Guti, a great apostle of the Gospel, had built many churches in Africa, and at the time we met him, he was supervising two thousand pastors with a total of one million members. Dr. Horner introduced us to Dr. Guti who took a liking to us and invited us to visit his country to conduct a healing crusade.

John and I were delighted to have this ministry opportunity. We had to pay our own way there, but all of the other expenses were taken care of by Guti's ministry, Forward in Faith. Not only did we raise money to travel to Zimbabwe, but we also invited a team of persons to travel with us. In addition, we raised enough money to purchase a computer, printer, and other office equipment to give to the ministry of Dr. Guti. While there, we held a week-long healing crusade, and many people were healed. At the end of the crusade, Dr. Guti also prayed for John and his call from the Lord to go from East to West. When I think about it now, the ministry trip to Zimbabwe was a sign of God's promise to John and the beginning of God's calling to send John from "East to West."

At Lake Junaluska, John and I met three important people who were directors at the Upper Room, a central publishing arm of the United Methodist Church in Nashville, Tennessee. The Upper Room publishes the Upper Room Daily Devotion magazine as well as many other books. It is one of the main spiritual and educational hubs of the entire United Methodist Church.

During this time, John was still teaching in the public school. In the summer of 1992, John requested and received an application for the position of Director of Spiritual Formation and Healing. The application was very involved and asked questions requiring several pages to answer. As he was working at the computer to complete the application, two spiritual Christians called John to say they were praying for him because they felt that he was the person for the position. We definitely were amazed because they had not been told that John was applying for the position. Others, as they heard that the position was available, began to call from across the nation to tell John they were praying that he be accepted for the position.

Later, we attended a conference about an hour from our home. At that conference was a United Methodist minister, Dr. Teri Teykel, a powerful man of prayer. After one of the sessions at which he spoke, we had an opportunity to talk to him during lunch. I like to think that God arranged all of this. It gave John an opportunity to discuss with a colleague who had an understanding of the spiritual things of God, including healing, and also share his possibility of working at the Upper Room. Dr. Teykel listened intently; then he said, "You will be going to the Upper Room." We realized that Dr. Teykel was not just speaking his own words, but he was speaking what he heard from the Lord. Then he said,

"Surround yourself with people who will pray for you." Stunned by his words, we sat there in silence. You would think that now that we had heard a *rhema* word from God, things would really begin to happen. This, as they say, is the rest of the story.

Along with others, I continued to pray fervently for John to be accepted for the position of Director of Spiritual Formation and Healing. After submitting his application for the position, John was invited to the Upper Room for an interview. The interview seemed to go well. John's hopes were high, but he did not hear anything concerning the position. Several months passed, and in 1993, John received a letter saying that they had hired someone else for the position. We were most perplexed, to say the least, but we just released it all to God, believing if God did not open up this position for John, God must have something better in mind. We could have become upset and distraught, but we chose to believe and trust that God knew what God was doing. About two months later, John was invited to go to Nashville to participate as a consultant for spiritual guidance in matters pertaining to the Upper Room. At the time, several directors who were a part of the hiring process became better acquainted with John.

Later, as John was being driven to the airport, he mentioned to one of the supervising directors that he felt God still had something for him in the Upper Room ministry. The director said, "It's funny that you should say that because the position we just filled that you applied for has unraveled." Amazed, John asked that if the position was open, he be given a second look.

We didn't hear another thing until the end of February 1994. Then suddenly, in March, John was asked to come to Nashville for another interview before a committee.

From East to West—A Miracle That Takes Its Own Time

John was required to take a psychological exam before being given final approval for the position. We were very concerned about this because a Jewish psychologist had given John a psychological exam in Delaware that proved to be a very unpleasant experience. The psychologist refused to believe that John could forgive his father for leaving the family. John had been able to do so because of the grace of God in Christ. Still, the psychologist insisted he couldn't have done so. Fortunately, the psychological, test at the Upper Room went well, and finally, in April 1994, John was offered the position of Director of Spiritual Formation and Healing. This indeed was the fulfillment of God's Word, spoken to him over twenty years previously. In this new position, John flew all over the country, literally from "East to West," teaching, preaching, and praying for those seeking God's love and presence for spiritual healing of their minds, bodies, spirits, and relationships. John taught across denominational lines. He taught in Cuba for a week and also traveled to Africa, not once but twice, to teach other pastors and God's people the healing love of Christ.

From this example we see that a miracle of God may take years of time to come to its final fruition, but in the meantime, we have the responsibility to pray, believe, trust, and have great patience concerning what God has spoken. When God speaks, it is our duty to believe that what God has spoken will manifest itself and become a reality in our lives.

Nine

The Importance of Forgiving as It Relates to Miracles

When we pray for God's miraculous work in our lives and don't see our prayers answered, we may feel that God has forsaken us. It's in those times we should examine our lives and determine whether we are doing something that may obstruct God's work in our lives. Often, we don't realize that the way we think or our own previous actions influence what is happening in our bodies. Some who have studied the relationship between the body and the mind call this the mind-body connection.

The Scripture points out that as a man thinks in his heart, so is he. How we think may even influence the miraculous work of God in our lives. Scientific research confirms more and more that these words are very true. It is a known fact that negative emotions of our minds, such as resentment, fear, anger, hurt, can cause reactions in our heart, kidneys, circulatory system, and immune system—in fact, all of the systems of our bodies. This can happen even when we are totally unaware of the anger or fear within us.

In his book, *Psychology, Medicine & Christian Healing*, Morton Kelsey, shares a statement by Dr. Jerome Frank, professor of psychiatry at John Hopkins University, from his book, *Persuasion and Healing:* "today's medical evidence suggests that anxiety and despair can be lethal, while confidence and hope are life-giving" (p. 205). Dr. Frank further states in the conclusion of his study, "faith may be a specific antidote to certain emotions, such as fear and discouragement, which may constitute the essence of a patient's illness" (Ibid.).

One demonstration of the mind-body connection can be seen in the autonomic nervous system which consists of the sympathetic and parasympathetic systems of the body. The sympathetic system causes a quick release of energy when we are faced with a situation that may be alarming. It prepares us for a flight or fight response. For example, if we encounter a dangerous situation, such as a wild dog or a bear, a chemical is discharged in the pituitary which alerts the glands. Morton Kelsey states: "Immediately the blood vessels to the stomach and intestinal area are shut down, Digestion, assimilation, and elimination all nearly halt, and blood driven from these areas is sent to the brain, lungs, and external muscles, where energy is suddenly required" (Ibid. p. 217).

In addition, heart and lungs produce more fuel, the liver releases carbohydrates, our blood pressure rises, and the clotting time of the blood decreases to prepare us for a possible wound. All of this release of energy prepares us to fight or flee from the situation. The problem is when we have emotions such as resentment, hostility, fear, or hatred, our bodies respond in the same way. In addition, this may occur even when we simply worry and the released energy is not utilized by the body. As so well expressed by Kelsey: "Unconscious fear and anger can react incessantly on our hearts and kidneys, our stomachs, the circulatory system, or the immune system without our knowing it, until the structure of one organ or another has been changed enough to cause pain" (Ibid. p. 218). Now, if instead of a beast, we produce this reaction to anger, fear, or worry, the energy that comes forth is not used by the body and reacts against the body.

Some physicians also recognize the effects of anger and anxiety on the body, specifically the heart. Referencing a British Medical Journal of February 1997, Dr. Julian Whitaker, states in his book, *Reversing Heart Disease*: "Researchers at Harvard Medical School determined that the risk of heart attack increased by 230 percent in the two-hour period following an episode of anger" (p. 283). Simply recalling a past incident of anger can cause an individual's "heart to beat erratically and the arteries to constrict in people with heart disease, reducing blood flow and bringing on the pain of angina" (Ibid. p. 283). This study and other such studies clearly make it evident that we should take seriously the words of Scripture: *"Get rid of all bitterness, rage and anger, brawling and slander, along with every form of malice"* (Eph. 4:31).

Howard Clinebell Ph.D., an internationally known counselor, teacher, and United Methodist pastor, in *Wellbeing*, points out that scientific experiments "have documented negative body changes from job loss, divorce, and bereavement, as well as positive body changes from getting a pet, meditation, psychotherapy, spiritual healing" (p. 49). Studies further reveal that hopelessness is an important factor in the onset of fear, cancer, and arthritic problems; and hopefulness is important to the recovery of such persons (Ibid.) To put it very simply, the mind influences the immune systems of our bodies, and the immune system talks back to the mind. Such interactions between the mind and body are most important in determining our health. One major emotion that both ministers of healing and medical doctors have observed as a major block to healing is unforgiveness.

Unforgiveness/Forgiveness

Unforgiveness, as it relates to our bodies, can bring about depression, anger, bitterness, and destructive behavior. Unforgiveness, just as the emotions of anger, resentment, and fear, distresses the central nervous system, the muscular-skeletal system, the glandular system, and also depresses the immune system.

Jesus said when we stand praying, we should forgive, so that our trespasses may be forgiven by the Father. When we come before the Lord asking in prayer, we must remember to come to God in the proper way. There are times when unforgiveness, as well as sin, affects the answering of our prayers. Sometimes, our prayers are not answered because we have too much unforgiveness in our hearts. Jesus said, *"Have faith in God...all things for which you pray and ask, believe that you have received them, and they will be granted to you. Whenever you stand praying, forgive, if you have anything against anyone, so that your Father who is in heaven will also forgive you your transgressions"* (Mark 11:22, 24-25 NASB. Many people become sick because of the bitterness and resentment they hold in their hearts. Continued bitterness and resentment can cause many diseases; continuous thinking in hateful ways toward others can occupy our minds like the repeated playing of a song or telling of a story. It goes over and over in our minds, affecting the chemistry of our bodies and eventually affecting our bodies in negative and harmful ways. This is true even when others have abused or mistreated us and we are justified in the way we feel.

The model prayer, known as the Lord's Prayer, given by Jesus to his disciples, also emphasizes a connection between our sins being forgiven and the forgiveness of those who transgress against us. Forgiveness toward others not only enables us to be forgiven of our sins, but is often the key to the healing of relationships, particularly the relationships between husband and wife, parents and children, and even supervisor and employees. Jesus, in his teaching, made it very clear that it is important to forgive. Jesus said, *"when you are offering your gift at the altar, if you remember that your brother or sister has something against you, leave your gift there before the altar and go; first be reconciled to your brother or sister, and then come and offer your gift"* (Acts 5:23-24 NRSV). Jesus also said we are to love and pray for our enemies. How often do we think about this and act on those words? Or, do we allow those thoughts in our minds to fester and grow until our bodies can no longer take it? Do we forget that James 5:16 states that we should confess our sins to one another and pray for one another that we may be healed? What a different world this would be if we put these words into practice. What different people we would be if we took these words to heart and acted on them. Years ago, I was privileged to coordinate a group of Christian women in our area to come together and pray as part of a larger group started by Dorothy Harris, an outstanding Christian lady from Philadelphia. After several months of getting together and working toward establishing a viable group, I came under unfair criticism from one of the group members. To this day, I don't know the reason for her negative comments toward me, but it brought me a great sense of hurt. I was so happy to have an opportunity to meet with other women in prayer, support, and fellowship I never saw it coming.

Later, I developed symptoms in my lower legs and ankles that appeared to be arthritic. Seemingly out of nowhere, my legs began to hurt. I began to pray and ask God to take away the pain, but nothing happened. I did sense in my spirit that God was encouraging me to exercise to relieve the pain, although I had never heard of exercising as a way to relieve arthritic pain. So, most mornings when I got out of bed, I exercised by running in place for ten minutes. This helped me to cope and relieved the pain I was feeling, but the next morning, it was there again. This went on for about a year.

The following year while attending a retreat, I decided to go into the meeting room before others arrived and get on my knees to pray. While on my knees, I was reminded of the person who had brought me hurt, and the Holy Spirit spoke into my spirit that I should forgive her. Without hesitation, I did forgive her, and as I did so, a beautiful anointing of the Holy Spirit came over me, as if to say the Lord was pleased. When I got up from my knees, I had no more pain in my ankles and legs. God had graciously healed me and blessed me to personally experience a miracle of instantaneous healing. Now, over twenty-five years later, I am still free of pain in my ankles.

When we forgive, we allow God's love and grace to flow into our beings and also into the situation that we are forgiving, bringing about God's blessings and answers to our prayers. But when we do not forgive, we block the love and flow of God's healing grace, and we block the flow of answered prayer. Sin in our lives works the same way to block the flow of God's love and healing grace. It's like a stream of water that cannot flow properly because it is clogged with twigs and other objects. The twigs and debris must be removed before the water can flow properly. Or it's like a hose that is clogged; the water cannot flow through it until the dirt and murky stale water is removed. This works just as well for the person who has caused hurt and needs to ask for forgiveness. We must be willing to ask God's forgiveness and the person's forgiveness, and put aside the sin. The choice is ours. If we are willing, God will help us. Sometimes, forgiveness is a process, like peeling an onion one layer at a time. But if we ask God to help us, we will be able to do it.

At times, we are faced with situations over which we have no control that deeply affect us in our hearts and minds. In such situations, forgiveness is often very hard to do, particularly when the other person has caused pain, abuse, or even death. Forgiveness in such situations may have to be a process over a period of time. In some cases we can only forgive with God's help and strength. Still, it is possible. For example, because they helped to protect Jewish people from the German military, Corrie Ten Boom and her family were placed in a concentration camp where her father and sister died. She spoke all over the world about how God enabled her to forgive those who were responsible for their deaths. We know that Joseph of the Old Testament was able to see a higher purpose in his suffering at the hands of his brothers. He was willing to forgive, and forgiveness brought forth restoration and healing and healing of relationships for both himself and his family.

What scientists and psychologists are just now discovering, God has always known. God knows that we need to forgive in order to live together in harmony and peace, with others and with ourselves. God has placed such an importance on forgiveness that God sent Christ, God's only begotten son, so we could choose to be forgiven of our sins and be whole and free from suffering. It is Jesus who said as he hung on the cross, *"Father, forgive them; for they know not what they do"* (Luke 23:34a KJV). Forgiving is not simply following the laws of God and the teachings of Christ; it is allowing ourselves to be rid of toxic thoughts that play over and over in our minds and, if continued over a long period of time, can be detrimental to our health.

Releasing others through forgiving them for what they have done to us can have far-reaching personal affects.

For example, John years ago, had an opportunity to teach a healing workshop on the importance of forgiveness and healing. During the workshop, he instructed those present to think of someone they needed to forgive and forgive them. As they did so, one of the ladies suddenly shouted out, "Look! My hands are opening." She had held unforgiveness towards her sister for twenty years. Her arthritic claw-like hands and fingers that were closed slowly opened up until they looked like normal hands. God, in Christ, right then and there chose to confirm in a miraculous way, the relationship between forgiveness and healing. Ephesians 4:31-32 reads, *"Get rid of all bitterness, rage and anger, brawling and slander, along with every form of malice. Be kind and compassionate to one another, forgiving each other, just as in Christ God forgave you.*" The more we are able to forgive, the more we will experience God's miraculous works in our lives.

Forgiveness in Marriage

It is my profound belief that if a marriage is to survive many years with love and happiness, the marriage must be one where each person is willing to forgive. No person is perfect or has perfect behavior in a marriage. Eventually, there is bound to be a conflict. There are three things that are most important in a marriage—respect and value for one another, meeting each other's emotional needs, and communicating with one another. Still, it is most difficult to be perfect in all those areas, all of the time. This is why forgiveness is of utmost importance. Not being a marriage counselor or a psychiatrist, I am limited in my expertise in this topic, but I do know what has worked in our marriage.

Early in our marriage, John and I learned to respect one another as we might respect any friend or person we know. When one spouse ridicules his or her spouse, in private or in the company of others, the result is hurt and pain. John and I agreed that we would speak well of each other in the company of others. When this did not happen, there would be a discussion later, and the offending person would ask forgiveness of the one who was offended.

We learned the importance of communicating our feelings, to each other and if the problem could not be resolved through simple discussion, prayer became an important and powerful tool to bring about healing and wholeness in our relationship. In his book, *Hope-Focused Marriage Counseling*, Dr. Everett L. Worthington includes a chapter titled, "Interventions for Promoting Confession & Forgiveness." Dr. Worthington stresses the importance of prayer and reflection on Scriptures by marriage partners together (pp. 139-140). In Dr. Worthington's discussion on loving communication, he states: "I believe that the root of all communication problems—whether they are understood as misunderstandings, poor communication styles, or attempts to gain power within the marriage—can be understood as a deficit of love" (p.66). He goes on to say, "Communication difficulties will not be dealt with unless the root cause of deficient love is addressed. Partners must defeat pride and power and replace them with love through valuing the spouse, even if it means laying down one's own expectations and rights" (p.66).

One thing that really perplexed me was the number of people we had known for a period of years, who were getting a divorce. It bothered me so much that one day as I was praying, I asked God to reveal to me why so many people, including my Christian friends or acquaintances, were getting a divorce. John and I were parents to three young children at the time, and I definitely didn't want division to come into our marriage. God revealed to me that it was not His will for anyone to divorce. God showed me that many times divorce is due to the attacks of the evil one. The evil one desires that marriages break up because (1) it is an affront to the will of God; (2) the family is the smallest nucleus of the Church, thus divorce affects the Church in a negative way; and (3) divorce greatly affects the lives of the children born to that marriage. So, when a divorce happens, it not only affects the married couple, but those around the couple, the children, and the Church—the people of God. Those who love the Lord and are married often find themselves not just having to contend with the everyday problems of life and the natural adjustments that married couples must make, but the attacks of the evil one against their marriage.

To have victory over these attacks, prayer must become an important part of the marriage. I remember the times in our marriage when conflict between John and me would cause hurt and a strong feeling of separation rather than togetherness. When I prayed about this, the Lord revealed to me that I must take authority over those things that were causing conflict. As I prayed, God would reveal those negative things, such as anger, pride, confusion, and disorder that were working against our marriage. I took authority over and prayed that they be replaced with the order, peace, love, joy, and harmony of the Holy Spirit. This was all done in the name of Jesus. When I first did this, I found that the situation changed immediately. I was convinced that what was happening in our marriage was truly initiated by the evil one. There were times when it took a period of time of prayer, but I can thank God that even those times did not last for weeks. It was and is truly the grace of God that has kept us together through over fifty-three years of marriage.

Most people have heard the expression, "The family that prays together stays together." As I look back at past situations, I realize more and more that prayer sustained John and me during our trials. We were very young when we had the most conflict in our marriage. Once John accepted Jesus as his Savior, much of the conflict dissipated. John became more tolerant of me, and because of the power of the Holy Spirit within him, he was able to resist the temptation to get angry and became much more forgiving of anything I did that irritated him. With God's grace, I continued to be patient in the strength of the Lord.

One Scripture verse that I have found to be very true says, *"In your anger do not sin. Do not let the sun go down while you are still angry, and do not give the devil a foothold"* (Eph. 4:26-27). When we don't forgive and hold a grudge, not speaking to one another for days, we are being destructive to our marriage. Such behavior allows anger to overtake us and rule our minds in what we say and think. In fact, when there is no forgiveness, we tend to play over and over in our minds the hurt we experienced, which in turn may cause us to become angrier and more bitter. If not dealt with, this anger and bitterness can actually cause harm to our bodies and/or our minds, as well as our marriage relationship.

Only God should be ruling our hearts and minds. Instead of giving the devil a foothold, we should allow God to come into the situation by praying together about the problem and coming to a resolution that is good for us. But, more than that, it is pleasing to God. John and I have dealt with problems that required us to pray together for weeks before they were resolved. As we have prayed together and allowed God to prevail in our marriage, we have seen God's miraculous power at work to keep our love fresh and our marriage a reflection of the grace of God.

Ten

The Miracle of God's Presence and Peace

As we walk this journey of life, there are times when we don't really recognize that Jesus is with us; we feel we are all alone even though we're surrounded by family or friends. It may be during those times when we are experiencing pain in our bodies or sickness in our lives. It may be those times when we face major crises, such as death of a family member, loss of a job, or financial difficulties. It may be when our children reject our Christian faith or choose a life related to drugs, crime, or associations with those who can lead them astray.

At these painful times, we should just stop and take time to remember the things that God has done for us. Remembering what God has done for us encourages us to continue the journey even though it may be difficult. Sometimes we forget who God really is. We need to remind ourselves of God's power and might. One important way to do this is through God's Word, just as Christ reminded the disciples of God's Word. Such a time happened as two disciples were walking on the road to Emmaus. In this account (Luke 24:13-34), the disciples walk with drooping shoulders to Emmaus, about seven miles outside Jerusalem. As they walk, the topic of their discussion concerns those things they have seen and experienced in the passing days—seeing Jesus handed over to the chief priest and scribes, seeing Jesus beaten and condemned to die, seeing Jesus crucified, then taken from the cross and buried. To top it off, they've heard from Mary Magdalene and the other women that Jesus is no longer in the tomb. They are confused and weary, to say the least.

But suddenly, Jesus walks with them and talks with them, they begin to experience a peace they had not known. At this time, they do not recognize who Jesus is. As Jesus walks with the disciples on the road to Emmaus, he reminds them of the Scriptures and teaches them their meaning. In the same way, we can remind ourselves, through reading and speaking God's Word that God is more powerful and more real than any sickness or pain that we experience. The study of God's Word should be something we do daily. When we meditate on God's Word and place this as top priority, we will find that we will reap many benefits. Those who meditate on God's Word are reenergized through God's love. They gain new strength to face the challenges and difficulties of life; they receive new revelations of God's wisdom and grace; and through God's Word they receive spiritual healing, physical healing, and more than that, God's peace. When we meditate on the simple truths and promises of God's Word, such as, *"The Lord is my Shepherd, I shall not want"* (Ps. 23:1 NASB) or *"The Lord is my refuge and my fortress"* (Ps. 91:2 KJV); we allow the light of God to come into our hearts, our minds, and throughout our bodies, bringing strength and hope. Such reading and study help us to come into the presence of God and allow God to give us the miracle of God's peace.

Note that once Jesus comes into the presence of the disciples, he meets them at the point of their need in the midst of their confusion and weakness. He begins to explain and give them an understanding of their concerns. In the presence of Christ, all worries cease, and the cloud of darkness that keeps us from focusing on the love of God is removed from our hearts and minds. Once again, we remember that Jesus is a friend who sticks closer than a brother or a sister. Once our hearts and minds are cleared, we are able to really listen to what God is trying to say to us. Once we focus on God and experience God's presence, we are no longer the same. We are changed; we are transformed.

As the disciples and Jesus continue to travel, they finally come to the edge of the village where they intended to go. Jesus appears to leave them, but they press him to stay for supper, for it is nearly evening. When he sits down with them, he blesses and breaks the bread. Suddenly, they are amazed, for they recognize who he is. At their recognition, Jesus disappears.

Sometimes it is in our fellowship with one another, as Christians, that we receive peace and truly begin to understand that Christ is still with us. We understand this when we break bread together in fellowship, as we pray for one another, and as we sit, talk and share the love of God with one another.

On the walk to Emmaus, the disciples realize that all along there was a witness to their spirits of the One who has walked with them, for they said to each other: *"Were not our hearts burning within us while he talked with us on the road and opened the Scriptures to us?"* (Luke 24:32).

The Scripture says that the Holy Spirit witnesses to our spirit that we are children of God (Rom. 8:16). Here the Holy Spirit witnessed to them that they were truly in the presence of Jesus the Christ, the Son of God. When we experience the presence of God, we know it, for our hearts are warmed within us and the peace of Christ lifts us to new heights.

The times when John and I have experienced the presence of God have usually been during times of meditation or prayer. We have discussed how we felt far more than the quiet embrace of the Holy Spirit during our individual prayer time. On some occasions of prayer, it is as if we are taken to another place beyond our cares and worries. In this spiritual place, there is no need to ask for anything because there is a special knowing inside of us that everything has been taken care of and all that really matters is that we are loved by God. There are no thoughts going forth, as in our usual prayer time, because there is a special oneness with God. Our hearts and spirits are completely connected to God.

Before Jesus began to journey with and talk to the disciples, they felt they had lost their hope of the Messiah. They had walked with him and talked with him, and now he was gone. At times many of us feel that way. At such times, we should stop and take time to sit and remember the things that God has done for us. As we remember God's love, God's blessings, and God's care, we will often find that the pain or sickness we feel, or the desperation we are experiencing seems to diminish. In their place, we experience the love, the presence, the peace, and the strength of the Lord welling up within us, giving us hope to go on, to believe we can be healed, giving us hope that all things are possible in Christ. Being in the presence of God is healing to our bodies, our minds, and our spirits. When we think about the loving grace of Jesus, we allow ourselves to open up to his presence and power. For the Christian, having a relationship with God is vital to our daily existence. There is power in the way we think and relate to God.

John Wesley spoke about his heart being warmed. After this experience, his life was not the same. He preached in a different way, he prayed in a different way, and he inspired thousands to turn to God. In the same way, the disciples were unable to keep all of the exciting things that had happened to themselves. Can you believe it? They are many miles outside of Jerusalem in their walk with Jesus, but in that same hour, they get up and return to Jerusalem and immediately tell the Eleven disciples and others with them what happened to them on the road to Emmaus and how Jesus made himself known in the breaking of the bread. Truly, it is a miracle that we can experience the presence of God, in Christ and know without a doubt God's presence and love.

One Scripture that speaks to the promise of God's peace is in Philippians 4:4-7: *"Rejoice in the Lord always, I will say it again: Rejoice! Let your gentleness be evident to all. The Lord is near. Do not be anxious about anything, but in everything, by prayer and petition, with thanksgiving, present your requests to God. And the peace of God, which transcends all understanding, will guard your hearts and your minds in Christ Jesus."*

This Scripture has meant a great deal to me throughout the years. Whenever I get into the mood of wanting to worry, I remember this Scripture, a step-by-step guide of what I should do to counteract worry. First, I rejoice that I have a God who is King of kings and Lord of lords, able to do all things. God is a God of the impossible and has power to do what I am unable to do. God created the Universe and is in complete control of all creation. When we worship and praise the Lord, we create an atmosphere that is inviting to the Lord; and when we come near to God, through our praises, God comes near to us. The simple act of praise lifts us up beyond our fears to a place in God's presence where we are able to see things from a different perspective.

Second, God has given us the privilege, through the authority of Jesus Christ, to bring to God all of our concerns, no matter how great or how small. Through Christ and his sending of the Holy Spirit, we are given the assurance that those who cry out to the Lord will be heard. God is definitely near us, for God has promised never to leave us or forsake us. We simply need to believe that God is able to answer our prayers, and God can work for good even those negative things that are happening to us.

As we praise the Lord and call upon God's name, God's peace stands guard over our hearts and minds. God's peace stands guard against the enemy of our souls, who desires to crush us with despair and cause us to be in deep depression and grief. God also guards our hearts and minds against anger that may lead to acts of retaliation and revenge against others. God guards our hearts and minds against thoughts of suicide and replaces those thoughts with words of hope and encouragement. It's so important that, as the Scripture puts it, we do not allow the devil to have a foothold in our lives (Eph. 4:27).

Once we have this peace, even if we cannot purchase a material gift for others, we can bring this God-given spiritual gift of peace to others. *It is a gift without price, for Jesus paid for this gift through his shed blood on the cross.* We can bring peace to others *through an encouraging word.* We can bring peace to others *through a listening ear.* We can bring peace to others *through God's love.* We can bring peace *through our prayers and intercessions.* As peacemakers, we give testimony to the world that we are sons and daughters of God.

Those of us who are blessed to acknowledge Jesus as our Savior must remember that *nothing can separate us from the love of God, nothing can separate us from the presence of God, and nothing can separate us from the peace of God.* This is a peace and reconciliation that Jesus gave to us through his shed blood on the cross. Remember, we may not have peace because of the world and its darkness, but because of Jesus Christ, we can have peace in our hearts and minds. Remember, Jesus is our joy; Jesus is our strength;

Jesus is our peace. If we allow Jesus to abide within us, he brings the miraculous peace that surpasses all understanding.

Recently, I experienced the peace of God that surpasses all understanding. In spite of the same challenges I faced, the same unsolved problems, the same lack of progress on certain projects, peace suddenly came over me like I seldom have experienced. The Lord's presence seemed so real that I could touch it. This peace lasted for at least two weeks and a degree of it still remains. God is good! God's mercies are everlasting and endure forever!

Eleven

Miracles Happen When We Listen to God

I am convinced that if we want to see more of God's miracles, as well as experience God's presence, we must take time to listen to God. Jesus made it clear that his sheep know and listen to his voice. Sometimes, knowing the will of God and listening to what he desires can appear quite difficult to us as humans. How is it possible to communicate with someone you do not see and seemingly cannot hear? But if we take the time, God will speak to us, even if it is in a still small voice. As we listen to God, it is important that we use the gift of discernment and make sure we are not listening to voices that have nothing to do with God. It is important also that we remember that God never tells us anything contrary to God's written Word in Scripture. In fact, God often speaks to us through the Scriptures.

Many find it difficult to hear from God, but the Scripture passage in John 10 lets us know there is something special about those who follow Jesus. Because Jesus is their Good Shepherd, those who follow him hear his voice. The sheep not only know the voice of God, they respond to the voice of

God. In fact, they hear God's voice and will follow no other voice. Their relationship with Christ is so close *they hear, they know, and they respond to his voice and will follow no other voice.*

Those who know about shepherding sheep also know that the shepherd has a special sound by which he calls his sheep. If they hear another sound, or even a sound given by another shepherd to his sheep, they will not come nor will they respond. They will only respond when they hear the sound their shepherd uses to call them. In Palestine, the sheep were used mostly for their wool, and over the years, the shepherds came to know and name each individual sheep (Barclay, *The Gospel of John*, vol.2, p. 56).

In the same way, Jesus knows each one of us so well and so intimately that he knows each one of us by name. Oh, what a joy to know that Jesus knows each of us by name! We know God called Moses by name when God spoke to him from the burning bush (Gen. 3:4). God called Samuel by name when he was still a young boy (I Sam. 3:2-14). The Lord called Martin Luther King Jr. by name and told him not to fear those who threatened him daily, but to stand up for righteousness, stand up for justice, and stand up for truth (Cone, *Martin & Malcolm & America*, p. 126). Jesus knows each one of us by name. Hallelujah!

But how can we follow the Good Shepherd and go with him all the way if we are not listening for his guidance and direction? Those who follow the Good Shepherd must listen and they must obey. Not only must we listen, but once we hear, we must follow the instructions given. Jesus said, *"If you love me, you will obey what I command"* (John 14:15). This is where listening and waiting on the Lord become so important, for how can we know how to follow and obey the Lord if we are not listening. Many times we cause our own problems because, even though we hear, we do not obey. To have the Lord's direction and guidance and to see God's miracles in our lives, we must take time to wait, listen, and obey. Amos 3:7 says, *"Surely, the Sovereign Lord does nothing without revealing his plan to his servants the prophets."* We are not all prophets, but all those who have accepted Jesus as the Lord of their lives should be able to hear and obey the voice of Jesus. I once counseled a young lady who was considering divorcing her husband. During the time of our conversation, she stated that the Lord had told her not to marry the person she married. I couldn't believe my ears and asked her to repeat what she said. She repeated that the Lord told her not to marry her present husband. This is an example of hearing the Lord, but not obeying.

Another important point in listening is those who want to hear from God must make themselves available to hear God. Most often, many of us rush through the day, from one situation to another, not having a clue that God is trying to get our attention. Have you ever felt, even while watching TV, that you should go and pray, or that you should go and read God's Word? This is God calling you to be in relationship. Once we make ourselves available, it is important that we take time not to just talk to God, but to listen.

When desiring to hear from God, we must expect that God will speak to us. God may speak through Scripture, God may speak through others, and God may speak through the Holy Spirit. Often the Lord comes in a still small whisper, just as God spoke to Elijah on the mountain. He was not in the wind, nor in the earthquake, or in the fire, but he spoke with a gentle whisper (1 Kings 19:11-12). When we don't listen for God's voice, we risk the danger of moving in the wrong direction or being influenced by others who are not listening to the voice of God. We can only follow God's direction after we take time to listen.

Often the problem is in listening. Some persons are like wolves in sheep's clothing; they pretend to have a relationship with God. When there is no relationship, in most instances, the person is not hearing from God. There are also those sheep who do not take time to listen to God, but are always in the front, giving their opinion. This leads to confusion, disorder, and distrust. This is also why, at times, the Church is in such confusion because there is no unity in discerning the voice of God. There are many times when we should pray before we speak. The Holy Spirit enables us to discern the voice of God from other voices in the world. This is why it is so important that we be in continuous prayer, so we will not be deceived and mistake other voices for the voice of God. We may even mistake our own thinking as the voice of God. Remember, we as sheep should only respond to the voice of God.

One day while John and I were attending a Christian conference in Orlando, Florida, we decided to take a late walk after the evening worship service. As we walked around the hotel, we met two friends who were also attending the conference. After a few minutes of conversation, I suddenly felt deep in my spirit that we should pray for our son, Stephen, who was over a thousand miles away, attending college in Hampton, Virginia. I shared this with our friends, and we then sat down at 2:00 a.m. to pray for our son. The next day, we learned that at that same time, Stephen was in a serious car accident that totaled his car. Thanks to God, he walked away from the accident unharmed. God had performed another miracle! Surely, the hand of God intervened in the life of our son. I thank God that I was sensitive to God's quiet voice, took the time to listen, and even in the midst of our conversation, was open enough to God's voice to sit down and pray. I also feel that being surrounded by Christian, Spirit-conscious friends made a big difference. We sat down immediately and prayed; we did not just pray, but prayed with expectancy that everything would be alright.

I am a firm believer that God gives us the desires of our hearts. If we truly want to hear from God, our desire will lead us to have a time of quiet and focus so we will be available to hear from God. Regular meditation, inviting the presence of the Holy Spirit, is vital to learning to hear from God and most important toward the manifestation of many miracles.

Twelve

Fasting into the Presence of God

John had a unique experience of fasting during the time he was a student at Oral Roberts University in Tulsa. He decided to go on a fast as a way of becoming closer to the Lord. His fast included no solid food, only liquids. He continued going to class, doing his studies, and even cooking for the family. I was amazed at how John was able to go day after day without eating any solid foods. He had a good disposition and was really quite pleasant.

John put it this way: "I was never in a position that was quiet enough or settled enough for God to do anything in me. I think this fast was a yearning, a prayer that I would be whole, able to respond to God's grace, God's love, God's presence. God said, 'OK. If you want to do that, there are some things that need to be adjusted in your life—there needs to be, perhaps, some repentance.' My prayer time was really intense—lots of weeping. It seemed there was some deep work that God wanted to do. It was a time for me to lay myself bare. I knew I was anyway, but you know how we try to hide from God and try to hold secrets. God was seeking my cooperation to work with Him at that deepest level of my need." ("A Conversation with John Penn," *Alive Now*, p. 27, March/April 2001).

During the forty days of John's fast, he was filled with God's joy and surrounded with God's presence. One day, after shopping at the grocery store, as he started to go home, it was all he could do to get home to be alone with the Lord. When he finally arrived, groceries were strewn throughout the house as he dashed to his room to be alone with God. Through fasting, John experienced the presence of God. In addition, fasting gave God the time and opportunity to transform and cleanse John from many things that would obstruct him from being made whole in his relationship with God.

It was through fasting that I finally received the confidence to go to divinity school. Years ago, my heart's desire was to serve the Lord, and I felt strongly it was to be through the ordained ministry. I had waited to go to divinity school because of my family; I wanted to make sure that my children were out of school and also to be sure this was what God wanted for my life. After all, it would take tens of thousands of dollars for me to attend a top school. My children had finished college and, to my surprise, my father—who had earlier said I should teach rather than preach—was now in agreement. To my amazement, my father sent me a check of one thousand dollars toward my tuition.

But going to school would take much more than one thousand dollars. It would take getting accepted to work on my master's degree in divinity, and it would take many more thousands of dollars. To my surprise, I was accepted by three schools: Vanderbilt School of Theology, International Theological Center, and Candler School of Divinity of Emory University. Still, I needed the finances.

Being quite impressed with Candler when I visited the school, I decided to apply for a scholarship. At the time, I was teaching music in the public school and needed to make a decision in time to resign my position before the school year was over in May. Still unsure of what I should do, I decided to fast. Previously, the longest I had fasted was seven days, and by the seventh day, I almost passed out. I knew that was not the way for me to go. I decided to fast for forty days, eating one vegetarian meal a day. For example, I would eat a salad with a baked potato for dinner. I asked the Lord to give me a sign that I should go to divinity school by being offered a scholarship. The period of fasting was during the months of February and March. As the days passed, fasting became easier, and I began to feel more and more at peace about attending divinity school, but still I did not have the money to go. I called Bishop Leontine Kelly, the first female African American bishop in a major Christian denomination. She emphatically told me she discerned that I should be in the ordained ministry. This encouraged me greatly, but I still did not have the finances.

Then it happened. After a month or two from the time of completing my fast, and only a few days before I needed to inform Candler if I was going to attend, I received a scholarship for half of the tuition. I was elated.

The first year of attending Candler was wonderful, although quite difficult. I had not gone to school for years, and I had many adjustments to make. I found myself in class with students twenty years younger; some were lawyers, and some had undergraduate degrees in religion. But God was faithful; God didn't bring me this far to leave me. Somehow, through prayers and trust in God, the Lord pulled me through with all As and Bs. The next year, I transferred to Vanderbilt to be closer to home. There was one disappointment because of this change. I had been asked to be an assistant to one of the professors, by making presentations/teachings related to teachings of the regular class. It was really an honor to be asked and something I would have really enjoyed. Then another miracle occurred that brought peace in the face of disappointment. All of my academic hours were accepted at Vanderbilt from Candler.

At Vanderbilt, the Lord continued to be with me, even blessing me with an invitation to speak to the students in a chapel service in 2002, a few weeks before graduation. What a miracle! After raising my children and teaching for over twenty years, I had, through God's grace and power, completed a master of divinity from one of the top schools in the country.

Fasting has been a way that both John and I have been able to come into God's presence, hear God's voice, and find spiritual healing or clear direction for our lives and the lives of our family. I thank God for the Holy Spirit who works in our lives through fasting and has sustained us during this process.

The Presence of Christ and His Healing Grace in Holy Communion

Another important opportunity we must not miss in experiencing the presence of God, in Christ, is Holy Communion. Here again, Christ is known to us through the breaking of the bread in his name. Holy Communion, also known as the Lord's Supper and the Eucharist, is one of the sacraments in most churches. In Holy Communion, we remember how because of God's love for us, God allowed God's Son to die for our sins. We remember not only the love of God, but also God's power that raised Jesus on the third day. Holy Communion, as the name implies, gives us an opportunity to commune with God. It is an opportunity that we must not take for granted. Holy Communion is more than observation of a ritual; it is a time of remembrance of what God, in Christ, has done for us. It is a time when we confess our sins with humble and contrite hearts. It is a time of giving thanks, as the word Eucharist implies, for what God has done for us and is doing. It is a time to experience the grace and presence of God, and if we believe that God is present during Holy Communion, surely God's presence, through fellowship with Jesus at the Lord's Table can bring healing to our minds, bodies, and spirits. But to experience this, we must have a sense of expectancy.

As I mentioned earlier, I was healed of a large cyst on my back during the time of receiving Holy Communion. The cyst was so large I had arranged to have it removed through surgery. After prayer from others during a prayer meeting and praying at the altar during Holy Communion, I felt deep in my spirit that I was healed. This was about a week before the scheduled surgery. In faith, I called the doctor's office and asked the nurse to cancel the surgery, even though the cyst was still present. She was startled by my request and couldn't believe it, but she canceled the surgery. Then an amazing thing began to happen. As each day of the following week passed, the cyst gradually reduced in size until it was completely gone by the day I had been originally scheduled for surgery. This taught me that sometimes it takes patience to see the goodness of the Lord. Holy Communion is a powerful source of God's healing love; we should never take Holy Communion lightly.

Thirteen

The Holy Spirit Miraculously Guides Us

God leads and guides us through the Holy Spirit in both simple and complex ways. How else can we discern the truth, both in the Church and in the world? Jesus said that when the Spirit of truth comes, *"he will guide you into all truth, He will not speak on his own, he will speak only what he hears, and he will tell you what is yet to come"* (John 16:13).

When we are full of the Spirit, we can discern the truth and we can even hear God speak the truth in our hearts. We not only know the truth when it comes to God's Word, but we are guided by the truth in living our daily lives. As said earlier, Jesus indicates in John, chapter 10, that he is the Good Shepherd and the sheep will follow him because they know his voice.

Years ago, when my children were small and I was a stay-at-home mother, I was prone to eat when I really didn't need to because food was more accessible. One day, I reached up to get a piece of cake that had been placed on top of the refrigerator. As I did so, I distinctly heard a voice inside of me say, "You don't need that." Now, I thought about it for a while. I even took the cake down and looked at it. I had a choice to make—was I going to be disobedient or obedient to the voice I heard? I decided to obey. As I look back, I'm sure it was the power of the Holy Spirit that enabled me to be obedient. I do believe that if I had ignored the nudge of the Holy Spirit, the next time, it would have been easier for me to eat other sweets, resulting in my gaining unneeded weight. I also believe that because I have been obedient, the Lord has led me in countless ways to understand how some foods can help me and others can harm me. For example, I have known for some time that green tea is good for the body. In addition, green tea has powerful antioxidants that help to reduce the risk of various kinds of cancer. God has blessed us with herbs and plants that not only satisfy our need to eat, but help to protect against deadly diseases and health concerns.

Years ago, I developed the habit of taking aspirin whenever I had a headache. One day, I heard the Holy Spirit distinctly tell me I should not continue taking aspirin. Now such advice is not necessarily good advice for everyone, but for me it was excellent advice. I have found that through simply saying a prayer, my headache usually immediately leaves. Not only am I blessed by the goodness of God, but I avoid the side effects of taking aspirin which I was not aware of. The side effects of taking aspirin were not known publicly at the time.

A powerful example of how the Holy Spirit guided the early disciples is found in Acts 16:6-10. Paul and the disciples with him had traveled throughout Phrygia and Galatia, for they had been prevented by the Holy Spirit from preaching the word in the province of Asia. They had come to the border of Mysia and tried to enter Bithynia, but the Spirit of Jesus did not allow them to do so. *"So they passed by Mysia and went down to Troas. During the night, Paul had a vision of a man of Macedonia standing and begging him. 'Come over to Macedonia and help us'"* (vv. 8-9). After Paul had the vision, he and the disciples immediately left for Macedonia. They were certain that God had called them to preach the gospel in Macedonia. So you see, God had a great purpose for not wanting Paul to go to Asia or Bithynia. Paul's going to Macedonia was the beginning of the introduction of the gospel to the Gentiles, resulting in thousands upon thousands of people, now millions, coming to know and accept the love of God in Jesus Christ.

Have you ever had the experience of the Holy Spirit leading you to a particular place? Yes, even in this day, the Holy Spirit will tell you where to go, what to do, and what to say. You may recall my account of God's guidance in the first chapter of this book. The Holy Spirit gave us clear direction not to stay in Little Rock, Arkansas but to continue on to the university, in spite of John's being extremely tired from driving all day. We must daily practice being in the presence of God through the Holy Spirit, so we can listen and discern what God is saying to us and how God is leading in our lives.

The Holy Spirit is not only the Spirit of Truth and our Guide, but also our Comforter and our Protector. The Holy Spirit gives us the strength to carry on and wisdom to know what to do in difficult situations. As we live our lives, we are often faced with many challenges that, no matter how we seem to pray, simply don't go away. Life can be like a bed of roses when suddenly we have that pain that just will not go away. Or, we walk in for our annual physical and find out that all is not well. We may be told that we have high blood pressure or we need surgery. Sometimes, what we are told is completely devastating. These are the times when we simply need to be still before God and allow ourselves to be aware of God's presence. It is the time when we should seek God's comfort and wisdom in the Holy Spirit. The Holy Spirit is the third person of the Trinity who is there when we are with the doctor, to give us encouragement in spite of our situation. The Holy Spirit is there as we go into the hospital and go through surgery, to comfort us, protect us, and guide the decisions of the doctors. The Holy Spirit is there in any crisis or challenge we may face in life.

What do you do when life throws you a curve? There are times when finances are not what we need them to be, or our supervisor is giving us a rough time. These are the times we should get by ourselves and seek the face of God. Remember, as said earlier the words of Philippians 4:6-7: *"Be anxious for nothing but in everything by prayer and supplication with thanksgiving let your request be made known to God. And the peace of God, which surpasses all comprehension shall guard over your hearts and minds in Christ Jesus"* (NASB).

The Importance of Professing the Word/Promises of God

If we desire to experience more of God's miracles, one way to do this is through professing and putting into action God's promises. God's Words are not empty letters on a page, but they are alive and active. This we note from reading Hebrews 4:12: *"For the word of God is living and active. Sharper than any double-edged sword, it penetrates even to dividing soul and spirit, joints and marrow; it judges the thoughts and attitudes of the heart."*

Here are just a few of God's powerful promises. As said earlier, just about the entire chapter of Psalm 91 is full of promises that I have relied on for strength, encouragement and healing in times of trouble and distress:

> **For protection:** *"He who dwells in the shelter of the Most High will rest in the shadow of*

the almighty. I will say of the Lord, 'He is my refuge and my fortress, my God, in whom I trust'" (vs. 1-2).

For healing: *"Surely he will save you from the fowler's snare and from the deadly pestilence...You will not fear the terror of night or the arrow that flies by day. A thousand may fall at your side, ten thousand at your right hand, but it will not come near you"* (vv. 3, 5, 7).

Other promises:

Proverbs 3:5-6: *"Trust in the Lord with all your heart and lean not on your own understanding; in all your ways acknowledge him, and he will make your paths straight."*

Matthew 11:28-30: *"Come to me, all you who are weary and burdened, and I will give you rest. Take my yoke upon you and learn from me, for I am gentle and humble in heart, and you will find rest for your souls. For my yoke is easy and my burden is light."*

Jeremiah 29. 11: *"'For I know the plans I have for you,' declares the Lord, 'plans to prosper you and not to harm you, plans to give you a hope and a future.'"*

Speaking God's promises to a situation not only builds our faith, but it brings life to the situation we find ourselves in. The Word of God and God's promises enable us to stand firm and continue to walk in the faith that God has given us. God's promises enable us to keep our focus on God's power and might, rather than the situation and circumstances we find ourselves in. There were times when John was in school at Oral Roberts University, neither of us had a job, and our income was insufficient to feed six small children. I found that I had to rely more and more on God. Speaking God's promises gave me the assurance and the encouragement that God would see us through and provide for us. Such promises included those found in Psalm 34:8-9: *"Taste and see that the Lord is good; blessed is the man who takes refuge in him. Fear the Lord, you his saints, for those who fear him lack nothing."* Or, *"I was young and now I am old, yet I have never seen the righteous forsaken, or their children begging bread"* (Ps. 37:25).

Reading and meditating on promises such as these gave me hope and encouragement to keep trusting and having faith that God would see our family through. During those years when John was in school, our family never went hungry. Even when we had very little, I learned to make delicious soups from leftovers, and we never found ourselves hungry. God kept us, even to the point of having a very nice home to live in. God is true and faithful to his promises. Following is an account of God's miraculous provision.

Miracles of God's Provision

These are signs of God's assurance that God has everything under control and provides our every need. At the beginning of this book, I related a fascinating account of God's provisions as we went on a nine-day trip to visit ORU in Tulsa. But God provides in so many other ways. For several extended periods of time, we had no health insurance, including two years after John resigned his teaching position in Wilmington, Delaware, to seek God's will and direction for ministry. Part of that time, John was in school working towards a theology degree at Oral Roberts University. God graciously provided us with good health, an astounding miracle for a family of eight. Another time was when we were preparing to come back to Delaware after John completed his degree. I had to leave my teaching position in Tulsa, and John had no teaching position until several months after we returned to Delaware.

In the months when we originally moved from Newark, Delaware to Tulsa, neither of us had jobs, and as a result, we did not have health insurance. I most certainly was concerned during these times; still, these circumstances provided an opportunity for me to completely trust in God and his ability and power to protect our children from harm and disease.

When we first moved to Tulsa and were applying for teaching positions, we quickly used up the little we had saved in about three months. The money we had from the sale of our home was placed on a lease purchase agreement to purchase our home. The sale of our home in Newark had been a whirlwind event. John was actually wall-papering and preparing the house for sale when a real estate agent knocked on the door and asked to see the house. We didn't even have a sign in the yard. The agent walked in as John was placing wall paper on the wall in the foyer. To our surprise, he said that he would buy the house and told John that he need not do any more to prepare the house for sale. Miraculously, our house was sold in less than a week with no sign in the yard.

In Tulsa, we had very little money to purchase food on a regular basis. About a year after we arrived in Tulsa, Mother visited from her home in Lorman, Mississippi, where she was a professor of education at the University of Alcorn. She brought a large box of different cuts of beef, and I was very pleasantly surprised. The cuts of beef were stored in our freezer and cooked sparingly for our family. After three months, only one medium-large roast remained. I debated whether or not I should cook it; finally I decided to take it out for a Sunday dinner. Anyone who walked into our home on that day would have thought that all was well as we sat around the dining room table with a nice large cooked roast. Just as everyone came to the table, ready to eat dinner with our last piece of roast beef, the doorbell rang. I quickly answered the door, and there stood Dr. Jerry Horner, a professor at Oral Roberts whom I wrote about earlier. His arms were full of something, though at that time, I had no idea what. I invited him in, and as he entered, he said, "We had a big get together last night, and we had all of this meat left. I decided to bring it to you." Believe it or not, he held at least three large shallow boxes, about three feet long and three feet wide, containing large, high quality hamburger patties. I was truly amazed that just as we were eating our last nice piece of meat, God directed someone to come over with more meat. Was this just a coincidence? I think not. God was truly revealing God's love and compassion, as well as the truth of the promise in Psalm 37:25b, *"I have never seen the righteous forsaken, or their children begging bread."* Dr. Horner had no idea of our needs for we had told no one.

As I shared earlier, I learned to cook the best tasting, filling and nourishing soup out of leftovers that I often placed in the freezer. To this day, I have a difficult time throwing out good food because I know the potential of what a little can do. In previous years, when shopping for our family, I purchased enough food to last almost a month; now I was down to shopping for three days at a time. God often gave us assurances that he was with us, in spite of the circumstances. One more account that I recall as a sign of God's assurance happened when John and I went shopping while we were at ORU. John usually went alone, but this day, we were together. While walking down the aisles at the store,

I looked down and saw a twenty dollar bill. I was elated; during that time, twenty dollars could purchase quite a lot of food. Then, I thought about the person who dropped it. Of course, I was tempted not to say anything, to just keep the twenty dollars. But, knowing that God would not be pleased, I went to customer service, explained that I had just found the money, and asked what I should do. The young man I spoke to advised me to leave it for about two weeks and if no one claimed it, I could have it. Sure enough, after two weeks, I made a point of returning to see if anyone had claimed the twenty dollars. I was delighted to learn that no one had, and the twenty dollars was turned over to me. I rejoiced at the goodness of the Lord and God's assurance that we need not fear, God would provide all that we needed.

One important way to stand firm on God's promises is to remember the great and mighty things God has done I could share many things, but one thing I would like to share is how God healed our son, John II. When he was about thirteen years old, his father was invited by the pastor of our church to take a special leadership training seminar at a retreat center in Aetna, Oklahoma, a small town outside Tulsa. Our entire family was excited because special activities were planned for the children. Everything went well until the third day, when someone was sent to the room where John and I were meeting. We were told that our son needed us. The children had earlier been taken to a pizza restaurant, where he started to have serious pain. We immediately took him to the emergency room of the small town. The doctor examined him, gave him some medication, and told us he had a stomach virus.

After taking the medication, our son continued to be in pain, so the next day, we took him back to the emergency room where we received the devastating news that John's appendix had burst. We were told they would have to operate immediately, or our son could die. At that moment, we began to pray and stand in the power of Christ for the healing of our son. After two days, we took John home, thinking that now he would be able to rest and recover, but after a few days, he continued to be in tremendous pain. We took him to the hospital where we were told there was a mass of infection about the size of an orange.

In the midst of all that was happening, someone in our family told me he had dreamed that our son died. I took this to the Lord in prayer, and the Lord told me this dream was not of God and I was to stand against the evil one who wanted to take the life of our son. I immediately took authority over those negative thoughts, and John and I continued to pray and believe that our son, John, would fully recover. When I look back now, I can see that God allowed this dream as a warning to me that the evil one indeed wanted to take the life of our child, and we were to stand against it in God's power and strength. John did recover and has become an outstanding young man. It was through persistent prayer and trusting in God and God's promises that our faith continued to be in action. God saw us through another crisis and in the process, performed a miracle.

Fourteen

A Day to Remember (When Miracles Don't Seem to Happen)

In 2010, without warning a pain began to develop in the area of my right leg behind my knee. It became so painful that I could not walk up or down the stairs in a normal manner. I literally walked with my hands on the stairs, to go up; to go down the stairs, I walked backwards. The pain was particularly annoying while I was driving and having to shift my foot from the accelerator to the brake. I became really concerned about driving, but was determined not to give up my activities at church. I attended our weekly women's prayer group as often as I could, refusing to stop. I continued to pray and drive, trusting that God would get me to my destination and return me safely to my home. Still, the pain was so bad that, at times, I felt slightly paralyzed in the entire lower portion of my right leg. Thank God for cruise control; without it, I would not have been able to drive more than five to ten minutes.

I then made a strong decision to really pray and meditate for my healing. I began to read Scriptures pertaining to healing. Within a few days, a nurse called to remind me that I was scheduled for a physical, which I had completely forgotten. While having my physical, I explained to the doctor my situation, and he suggested that I go to therapy.

After about a few weeks of therapy, my leg seemed much better, but later I was given a series of exercises to do that ended with five minutes of exercise on the cycle. The next day, I felt a strong burning sensation in the area behind my knee. All the next week it continued to hurt, even as we traveled to visit our daughter, her husband and children. I decided to discontinue my exercising until the pain subsided. Then, on the second Tuesday in January, as John and I were just about asleep, John said, "I really sense the strong presence of the Holy Spirit." Again he repeated, "I sense the strong presence of the Holy Spirit for healing." I prayed silently, as I knew that John was praying that my leg and tail bone would be healed. To my amazement, when I awoke there was no more pain in that area of my leg, but, after a day, my leg gradually began to hurt again. However, the brief relief of the pain gave me encouragement that my leg would soon be completely healed.

After several months of therapy, beginning in December 2010, and much more consistent therapy from February to April, I seemed to be making good progress with my leg; I was beginning to feel better and not having so much pain in my knee. Judy, my physical therapist, had previously been very pleased with my progress and gradually added weights to my ankles as I continued to do the leg exercises.

During the first Sunday of March, something that I never foresaw happened. We ministers on staff had just finished serving Holy Communion when Pastor Moore instructed two of us to serve those who were unable to come to the altar. We rushed around the church to three or four people in the congregation and those in the audio-visual area; then an usher told us that Brother Jesse needed Holy Communion. Brother Jesse was in the choir, right behind the pulpit area. I had to move quickly from the middle of the sanctuary to the back of the sanctuary and run up several steps. I took an unusually high step to the row where Brother Jesse was seated, but I soon discovered that I was not in the right place. So, I stepped down the high step on the leg with the painful knee. I immediately felt something rip through the side of my right leg, but I thought everything would be OK. Instead, within five or ten minutes of sitting down, the same leg began to hurt from the knee almost to the ankle. I hobbled home, and at my next therapy session, I was barely able to do anything. I continued to try to do the exercises without the weights. The next week, my therapist advised me she could no longer help me and I should go to an orthopedic specialist to find out what was truly wrong with my knee. She said, "Your pain keeps moving around." I responded, "The pain is not moving around, I sprained my leg and that is adding to the problem." This was now March 2011.

Knowing that I needed an MRI to find out what was truly wrong, I made an appointment with an orthopedic specialist. After examining me, he thought I had a meniscus tear and insisted I take another set of X-rays, although previous X-rays did not show the root of the problem. I did not want another X-ray, but I finally took the second X-ray at the doctor's insistence. These X-rays also did not reveal the problem with my knee.

The doctor finally sent me to have an MRI, as I had earlier suggested. He also advised me that the kind of sprain I had would take about six months to heal. When I returned to the doctor's office for the results, he informed me the MRI indicated that I did not have a meniscus tear but the beginning of arthritis. I responded, "The beginning of arthritis and it hurts like that?" He said yes and further advised that I have a steroid injection to help with the tremendous pain. I immediately replied, "No." I had read many things about the side effects of steroids and wanted no part of them. I did ask the doctor to write down the name of the injection, and I would think about it. What I really planned to do was to look it up and pray about whether or not I should proceed with the injection. I have a dear friend who has been through many therapies for her knee and none of them have really helped her, including treatment with steroids. I wanted to be sure of what I was allowing to have done to my knee and my body. The doctor had the name of the injection written down for me.

When I arrived home, I went to my computer, anxious to see what this injection was all about. My doctor had told me I would only need one injection, but the information indicated that most often the patient would need one injection every three or four months. I also learned after a period of injections with this steroid, the arthritis would become worse and the bones would be damaged. That was enough for me. I decided, with no hesitation, not to have the steroid injection. My trust would be in the Lord.

While I continued to pray and believe that God would work out a way for me to be healed, something most unexpected happened. On the first Sunday of April, as I was getting on my knees to pray while in the pulpit area, I felt a ripple go across my back. I wondered what it could possibly be, but thought that nothing would come of it. During the next two weeks, I found myself in excruciating pain, particularly when I sat down and then tried to get up. It felt like spasms in my back, and I felt completely paralyzed and unable to move. Then the thought came to say the verse *"I can do all things through Christ who strengthens me."* At first nothing seemed to happen; the pain was so great that I couldn't move. I repeated` the verse and again tried to get up.

This time I was successful. After about three days of doing this, another verse was spoken in my mind to say: *"God has not given me a spirit of fear, but of power, love, and a sound mind."* As I spoke the verse, I placed emphasis on the word *power*. Immediately, I was able to get up. Gradually, the pain subsided, and after two weeks, the pain completely went away. The God of mercy had healed me again. It proved to be true that the Word of God is more powerful than a two-edged sword. My knee was still in pain, but I was encouraged that God would certainly bring about a complete healing. I was still in pain in May 2011, when I was ordained an Elder in the AME Church.

I investigated other ways to relieve pain, but they were not covered by insurance. Finally, after more prayer, the Lord led me to essential oils for pain. I was quite excited when I went to the health food store, purchased several essential oils, put drops of each together with carrier oil, and started to put them on my leg and knee. I began this in July, one month short of a year of being in pain with my knee. I immediately saw a difference in the oil treatment compared to the eucalyptus lotion that I had been using. The Lord, through natural means with the guidance of the Holy Spirit, gave me the wisdom to put the oils together. This gave me the ability to cope with the pain.

Later, John and I went on vacation to Colorado. I had much trepidation about being able to travel, because when we went to California to see our granddaughter graduate, we had a change of planes in Phoenix. I had to be transported by cart from one gate to another. I wondered how I could go on a vacation that required walking and standing for some length of time. John encouraged me to go. While on the trip, we visited several places in Colorado Springs, including Garden of the Gods, the Seven Falls, the Air Force Academy Chapel, as well as shopping. With daily application of the essential oils, I was able to walk and stand much longer than I thought possible. After a week, we returned home from a great vacation.

God gave me a way out of the pain with a natural oil therapy. My healing was not complete, but I had less and less pain, and I looked forward to a complete healing in the future.

After leaving the therapist, I continued to pray, trust in God and do most of the exercises. During the last months of 2012, I was able to drive with less pain in my knee. Then in January 2013, without fanfare, I suddenly realized that I had absolutely no pain in my knee. I stood in wonder and amazement that I had no pain and decided to test the healing by running around the house for 15 minutes. Sure enough, I had no pain. Finally, in April of 2013, I discovered that I could walk a mile without pain. What a mighty God we serve—miracles do still happen!

Our Grandson Comes Home

To explain the events of our grandson, Giovanni, returning to our family, I must begin with the tragic account of our daughter Jacqueline's passing. We learned that Jacqueline was very ill while she was living near San Diego, California with her three young children, Eric, Christina, and Giovanni, who was about 8 months old. The symptoms of Jacqueline's illness began with excruciating pain in her back. When she finally went to the doctor for the pain, she was told she had a fracture, and no other tests were given. Later, she went to another doctor, who examined her eyes because she had blurred vision. He thought that she had a tumor, but still no further tests were given. When she called to tell me this, I became highly upset that she was so ill and the doctors had given her no further tests. It turned out that this was because of the type of insurance she had.

I called the doctor who said she might have a tumor to ask why he had not ordered any further tests. He agreed to do so on the coming Monday. Jacqueline went to another doctor, who after examining her, informed her that she had cancer and gave her only six months to live. *How could this be?* I wondered. Jacqueline was a young lady, only thirty-three years old. How could one so young have such a devastating disease? Although I know better now, I had never heard of anyone around Jacqueline's age becoming ill with cancer.

When I talked with the doctor by telephone, he first responded that he didn't know. He suggested that perhaps her pregnancy contributed to the problem because it caused more estrogen to develop in her body and too much estrogen in the body may contribute to the formation of cancer. We soon found out that Jacqueline's cancer started with a breast tumor that metastasized to other parts of the body. This was why she was experiencing pain in her back. She had months earlier told this to the doctor who gave her prenatal care. He told her that since she had been pregnant and was nursing her newborn baby, she could not possibly have a tumor.

A month after hearing Jacqueline's diagnosis, John and I decided to go to California and find out what was going on with our daughter. In December, we made the long airplane trip from Tennessee to California. Some of Jacqueline's friends had paid for her to enter a health center that advocated a raw food diet with wheat grass for healing the body. Her close friend, Sandra, went to assist her at the clinic. Her friends paid for her to stay at the clinic for two weeks, where Jacqueline resided in a nice, one-bedroom townhouse. While I was there, Jacqueline's pain grew severe, so we took her to the emergency room of a nearby hospital. There, after hours of waiting, the emergency room doctor confirmed that she had cancer, but gave no suggestions concerning how to relieve the pain.

With the diagnosis, we decided to bring Jacqueline home to Tennessee so we could better care for her. We made arrangements for her two oldest children to live with their father, from whom Jacqueline was separated. Sandra agreed to keep Giovanni.

I was not willing to give up the fight for Jacqueline's life. I believed, as did John that nothing is impossible with God, that if we believed and trusted in God, our daughter would be healed and made whole. When we brought Jacqueline home, she was extremely weak and could barely walk. She had to be helped up the stairs to the bedroom and could not open the door to the dryer to dry her clothes.

During this time, someone sent us *Why Christians Get Sick*, by Rev. Malkmus. It was an encouraging and informative book, giving more information on the importance of diet in maintaining and keeping our immune systems strong. Rev. Malkmus spoke of the importance of juicing, particularly carrot juicing and taking barley green. We read many testimonies of healing through the diet of eating raw foods and juicing.

In addition, I began to read other books concerning the benefits of juicing vegetables with a healthy vegetarian diet and how some people had greatly benefited from this type of diet. I felt strongly directed by the Holy Spirit that this was the way to help Jacqueline strengthen her immune system and possibly fight off the cancer. John began to diligently juice organic carrots for Jacqueline to drink, and we began to see good results. She gradually regained her strength, took daily walks, and washed her own clothes. We rejoiced to see her progress. Still, she complained about her back hurting, so we decided to take her to the hospital.

The doctors gave her no hope, but offered to give her radiation treatments to help with the pain. Jacqueline was given a room in the hospital and scheduled for a series of ten treatments. She became very distraught over her hair falling out and her skin looking like it had been baked in an oven.

While Jacqueline was in the hospital, I went to see her on a regular basis. One day, the doctor asked me if I would approve giving Jacqueline a steroid. I refused. I had read some disturbing things about steroids and did not want Jacqueline to experience the side effects of such drugs.

The next day when I came to the hospital, I couldn't believe what I was seeing. Swollen all over from head to toe, Jacqueline looked like she had been blown up like a balloon. I asked her what happened, and she replied, "They gave me a steroid, but they aren't going to do it anymore." Needless to say, I was very upset, particularly since the doctor had asked me and I said no. Then I realized that they didn't have to get my permission. Jacqueline was an adult and could give her own consent. They probably felt I was an overly protective mother who didn't know what she was talking about, and they really didn't need my consent.

After ten days, we brought Jacqueline home from the hospital and continued to try to build up her immune system through carrot juicing, a vegetarian diet, and supplements, such as a high quality aloe vera juice, shark cartilage, and vitamin C. Jacqueline received a letter from a lady who had cancer and should have died years earlier, but because of diet and nutrition, she had lived many years past what the doctors predicted.

In spite of the radiation that took a great toll on Jacqueline, the diet continued to help. Then the radiologist said she wanted to give Jacqueline more treatments. This I could not comprehend, particularly since they said the radiation would do nothing to treat the cancer and Jacqueline looked so burnt and swollen. I asked for an appointment with the radiologist to explain why additional radiation was needed. She agreed, but when I went to the hospital to meet with her, she never

A Day to Remember (When Miracles Don't Seem to Happen)

appeared. Later, I asked her, by telephone, what happened. Without any explanation, she responded, "If you don't want her to have the radiation, she doesn't have to have it." Was it just to get more money that this doctor wanted to proceed with more radiation? It may be difficult to believe, but it seemed to be true.

Jacqueline continued to do well while staying with us. She was able to climb the stairs, wash her clothes, and even take walks. Still, she longed to go back to California, so she could continue to be with her children, including Giovanni. Although Eric and Christina were now with her in our home, a judge in California said she could keep the children out of the state away from their father for only six months. She did not want to leave them with their father, so she decided to return to California. In May, after living with us for about six months, she returned to California.

Several times a week, I talked to Jacqueline by telephone, and she constantly told me things were going alright. However, it was a very stressful time for Jacqueline. She was regularly being taken to court by her ex-husband who was trying to take the children from her. He used her sickness as an excuse to do so, though he had never given her any money to take care of them.

When Jacqueline called in early September, the first words out of her mouth were: "Mommy, please forgive me." I was quite startled to hear her say that and asked, "Forgive you for what?" She explained that she had not been going to the doctor as she should have, and she had not been juicing or taking her supplements. After about three months, she finally went to her doctor. The oncologist told her that the cancer had spread to her brain and a nurse from hospice would soon be with her. This devastating news came about a month before her birthday. John decided to go and to see her for her birthday, and they had a very meaningful time together. He then flew back home and immediately prepared to go to Brazil to of all things, minister and teach about the healing grace of God.

While John was still in Brazil, Jacqueline's friend Sandra called to tell me Jacqueline was dying. The call came on a beautiful Sunday, in 1998, right after I had returned from church. I asked to speak to Jacqueline and told her that I loved her. I told her I was going to go to divinity school and spend the rest of my life serving the Lord, as I knew she had wanted to do and my mother, before she died, had also wanted to do. I could almost see and hear Jacqueline smiling over the telephone. She seemed to be at peace and ready to meet the Lord, even as her body was racked with this terrible disease. Later that day, she passed. Her ex-husband gained custody of Christina and Eric. Before Jacqueline died, she asked Sandra to take care of Giovanni, and Sandra graciously agreed to do so. We respected Jacqueline's wishes and allowed Sandra to keep Giovanni.

John made a trip to California to visit three-year-old Giovanni, who was called "John" at that time. John seemed to be a happy and well-adjusted child, but a few years later, when John was seven, Sandra called to say that she needed help with John. She asked if we would be willing to take him, and I agreed. We were living in Delaware, so I suggested that we meet about halfway since Sandra's husband drove a semi-trailer truck and was constantly travelling across the country. She promised to get back to me when this could be arranged.

Somehow, I had always felt that John would one day return to his family, but I never expected what occurred next. We never heard from Sandra, as expected. When I tried to call, there was no answer, and for four years, we had no clue about where John was.

A Day to Remember (When Miracles Don't Seem to Happen)

In 2007, out of nowhere, I received a call from Sandra. She again asked if we would take John, stating that it had become very difficult to care for him under her present conditions. Once again, I immediately agreed. John and I decided we could have him come to live with us in October, but because my father died early that month, John's arrival had to be delayed, for another month.

Finally, near the end of October, we met John at the airport. He was a nice-looking kid with an afro and cowboy boots. After quite a process, we got John enrolled in school. Beginning school about three months late proved to be quite an ordeal for him. Coming from Arizona, he looked and dressed differently, making him a standout target for the other kids who grew up in the East. That was a difficult year for John, as he tried to adjust to a new school situation. We had to go to the school at least three times to discuss his playing around during instruction time. During the previous summer and part of the school year, he had been traveling with Sandra's ex-husband and had not been in school. We were sure this affected his discipline when it came to school. He was a good child at home, but was having problems in school. Finally, we took him for counseling and the therapist told us he was a charming child, but needed time to adjust and transition from his previous situation.

The next year, we moved to a very nice area in Georgia with excellent schools. We constantly worked with John and encouraged him. He made good progress in school that year, making the honor roll for the entire year. He adjusted well to the community we lived in and made lots of friends. John really enjoyed science and progressed well in math, thanks to an excellent math teacher who constantly encouraged him. His homeroom teacher voted him the most creative student in class.

At the end of his fourth grade year, my daughter, Christina, asked us to allow John to come to live with her family. I was reluctant to let John go since he was beginning to do so well in school and was gradually making a good adjustment. But Christina insisted, using the arguments that the earlier he would be with them, the better and Jacqueline had asked her to keep John before she died. Christina was not able to take John when Jacqueline first asked because she was still in college and didn't have a job. Now Christina and her family had a stable income, and she felt more capable of taking care of John. Her husband, Damien, agreed with her, so I finally agreed, as well.

John went to live with Christina, Damien, and their three children (now four with a new baby). In January 2010, Christina and Damien adopted John, who has returned to using his birth name, Giovanni. However, for the last two years, Giovanni has lived with John and me to be in a better school situation. It is amazing how God, when we trust, works out the most difficult situations.

God has truly blessed Giovanni's sister, Christina, and his brother, Eric, even though their mother is deceased and they lived most of the time without an active father. They endured more than we ever dreamed of. Their father remarried, but there was very little relationship between them and their stepmother, and most of the time their father was not at home. At the beginning of the recession, they lost their home and were homeless for several months until neighbors took them in. The stress of everything led to Eric making very poor grades. Eventually he went to live with his other grandmother in Philadelphia. John and I were unaware of all that had happened to them, but we regularly lifted them up in prayer, and we know that it was the grace of God that saw them through.

Christina and Eric are now in college. We had the great pleasure of attending their graduations. Christina graduated from high school in Southern California, with honors; a year later Eric graduated from high school in Philadelphia with high honors and a scholarship to Stanford University where he is now completing his fourth year. Christina is studying to complete her degree in Fashion Design and Marketing. The rest of the story for Giovanni remains to be told, but God certainly worked many miracles in the lives of these three grandchildren—Christina, Eric, and Giovanni.

God Miraculously Uses What We Have

God is the creator of miracles. As the Scriptures reveal, with God, nothing is impossible. Only God can bring about miracles, but, I truly think it is possible for us to create an atmosphere or environment for miracles to happen. Years ago, I felt that God wanted me to have my heart's desire to start a business. After some time of prayer, I decided to begin a business featuring skin care and health care products. As a young teenager, I had a lot of problems with my skin breaking out, and although I scavenged everything I saw in my parent's medicine cabinet, nothing seemed to permanently help.

I joined a multi-level company that sells skin care products featuring aloe vera and began to see lasting improvement of my skin. Through this introduction to aloe vera, I began to realize the importance of natural ingredients. As I researched what the natural qualities of God's plants could do to heal the body, I had a special sense that I wanted more people to know the possibilities of healthy skin and bodies through the natural creations of God.

When John and I started in 1989, the business seemed to be making gradual upward and consistent progress. Then the recession came in the early nineties, and although I was able to pay the bills of our very small business, we were not making a profit. We even wrote a business plan and went to the Small Business Association. The man who interviewed me said our business was further along than most he had seen, but we did not get a loan. Both John and I were teaching and taking care of a family of six children, leaving me very little time to put into the business. Then I resigned my teaching position and decided to just work in our business. In May of that year, I sold $3,000 in products, working part-time and with only five skin-care presentations. It was then that I knew we had good products; we just needed to know how to market them. But no matter where I turned for help in marketing our products, people seemed to be only interested in what they could get out of it for themselves, not in helping us move forward. We got a lot of promises, but no action.

I looked at the big companies who didn't have any better products than we had, yet they were making millions of dollars. In fact some of their products were mostly chemicals. Although I wanted to have an all natural product, it was very difficult trying to convince my manufacturer to produce a product free of all chemicals. Most of our products were seventy to eighty-five percent natural. Our entire line of skin care was originally aloe vera based. As I was praying about our lack of marketing funds and how to get the needed consultants, God very distinctly told me, "Use what you have." Those words have kept me going with this business even though our profit was little or none. It is my belief that as I continue to trust in God and use what I have, God is going to perform many miracles through our business.

Jesus demonstrated in powerful ways how God can take the little we have and do great and mighty things. One illustration is the account of Jesus feeding the five thousand with five loaves and two fish that his disciples retrieved from a boy. This account is found in all four Gospels. Jesus told the disciples to have the people sit down on the grass in groups of hundreds and fifties. Then Jesus took the loaves and, looking up to heaven, gave thanks, blessed and broke the loaves and gave them to his disciples to give to the people. Jesus also divided the two fish among those present. When all had eaten and were satisfied, the disciples took up twelve baskets full of broken pieces and fish. The number who had eaten was about 5,000 men, not counting women and children (Mark 6:39-44). So, with just five loaves and two fish, given by a young boy, Jesus fed over 5,000 people. We see that Jesus is able to take our little bit and make it more than what we can dream or think. This miracle gives me hope that God will show us how to take the little we have and make it much more than we could ever imagine.

Fifteen

Faith, Mover of Limitations, Catalyst of Miracles

Faith is the energizer that leads to victory. Faith is the motivator of action. Faith is the catalyst of miracles. Faith is so important that God often refuses to bless us unless we have faith to believe and trust that God is able to do all things. As Scripture reveals, *"without faith it is impossible to please God."* God has given us examples through God's Word of what it means to walk in faith and trust in Him.

One of these great examples is seen in the life of Abraham. We know that Abraham acted in obedience and stepped out in faith to obey the call of God. Just as God was pleased with the active faith of Abraham, he is pleased with us as we use our faith.

One of the greatest challenges that Abram faced was the challenge to believe he would have a son as God had promised. In the fifteenth chapter of Genesis, God tells Abram to go outside and behold the heavens and count the stars, if he is able to do so, for his descendants will be as numerous as the stars. As Abram and Sarai increased in age, this was most difficult for them to believe. Although Abram believed, because so much time was passing and the promise had not been fulfilled, there was still doubt. They even tried to work it out in their own way. At the age of ninety-nine the Lord appeared to Abram and confirmed his covenant. It was then, his name was changed to Abraham and Sarai's name was changed to Sarah (Gen. 17:1-2,5, 15).

Faith and obedience are important to creating an atmosphere for miracles. First, we must believe that God is able to do all things and is the rewarder of those who seek God. In Genesis 18, Sarah laughed after being told by the Lord that she would have a Son. They were visited by three men (v.2), two of the three men were angels and one was the Lord. The Lord responded to her laughter by asking, *"Is anything too difficult for the Lord?"* (14a NASB) The answer is "No, nothing is too difficult for God."

We need to ask ourselves today: "Is anything too difficult for the Lord?" The Lord, continued, *"At the appointed time, I will return to you, at this time next year and Sarah shall have a son"* (14b). As the Lord prophesied, Sarah did have a son and named him Isaac. What a miracle! Abraham was one hundred years old, and Sarah was ninety (Gen. 17:17).

Now, you may say, "Come on, we're living in the modern age. People don't believe in things like this today. Furthermore, things like this don't happen— a person who medically cannot have a child having a child?" Let me tell you about persons I know who, medically speaking, were not supposed to have a child. Several years ago, at a family reunion, I met a lady who had been pronounced by doctors to be medically unable to have a child. In spite of this, she and her minister husband were expecting a child. Also, I personally prayed with a young lady named Carol, who came to our prayer group and tearfully told us that she had a miscarriage and was told by the doctor that she would never have another child. Believing that God could do the impossible, I led in prayer that God would bless her with a child. About a year later, she became pregnant and had a son.

When John went to Uganda with a ministry group, he ministered and prayed for the sick, including about five thousand persons in a large, open field. John had an opportunity to pray for many of those who attended the worship service. One of them was a lady who requested prayer for what John thought was the opening of her ears. But the African lady insistently kept repeating, "open, open." John realized, with someone's help, that she was requesting prayer not for her ears, but that her womb be opened. John had never had such a request in those words to pray for someone to have a child. Still, he did pray.

When John returned, he wondered if those prayers were answered. God set the stage to give John an answer. A short time after he returned home, John was approached by a young couple at his church where he was assistant pastor. Although they had one child, they had been trying to have another child for three years and requested prayer from John that they have another child. John prayed for them and believed with them that they would have another child.

Just as he had prayed for the lady in Africa, he did not know whether or not his prayer was answered. Then something unusual happened. Our daughter, Christina, decided to answer an ad for a babysitter. It was only after she interviewed for the position and told us who the parents and the child were that John realized this was the same couple he had prayed for in church nine months earlier. Amazingly, God chose that way to let us know that John's prayer was answered. Immediately, John had a special knowing in his spirit that this also related to the lady he had prayed for in Uganda. He knew this lady also had the child she so desired. God, at times, does choose to give us our heart's desire in miraculous ways.

If we want to see God do the impossible, it is our responsibility to activate our faith and step out in faith to do those things we are called to do as God's disciples. We cannot truly call ourselves disciples of Christ if we do not answer his call to believe. As we pray, we can also be bold in the things we know God wants us to do. In boldness, we believe for our friends, our church, and even for those we may not know. The Scripture says, *"Faith by itself, if it has no works, is dead"* (James 2:17 NRSV). If we are truly people of faith, we bear the fruit, which is our works, to show as signs of our faith. But we can only bear fruit as we boldly step out in faith without fear.

You see, brothers and sisters in Christ, it doesn't mean anything to know God's will if we are not obedient and if we have fear. Fear is like death in the bones. It is paralyzing. Fear refuses to let you do or achieve anything, and fear can be contagious if it is allowed to continue without stopping it in its tracks. *Fear brings in doubt and doubt can completely turn your heart and mind away from the things of God.* In James, we are told that God will give us the wisdom if we ask, and when we ask for wisdom, we must not doubt, *"because he who doubts is like a wave of the sea, blown and tossed by the wind. That man should not think that he will receive anything from the Lord; he is a double-minded man, unstable in all he does"* (James 1:5-8).

In order to please God, we must move out in faith, rather than shrink in fear. For example, you may have been afraid to buy your first car because you were concerned about how to get the money to pay for it, but your need for a car outweighed your fear. You may have been afraid to buy a house, thinking of all the responsibility, but your need or desire for a home outweighed your fears. Therefore, our need to please and obey God should outweigh any fears that will try to intimidate us and keep us from doing God's will and following God's plan.

To have faith and be able to see the miracles of God requires that we abide in Christ. He is the vine and we are the branches. Jesus said, *"If you remain in me and my words remain in you, ask whatever you wish, and it will be given you"* (John 15.7). With prayer and with faith *"we are more than conquerors"* (Rom. 8:37). There are many encouraging promises in Scripture that will strengthen us for our daily lives and for the tasks that God has instructed us to do as the people of God.

God has given us precious tools of prayer and God's Word, to enable us to walk in faith and to experience God's miracles. We must study the Scriptures, seek the Lord, and boldly step out in the things of God. God is faithful and will more than meet us as we step out in faith. As we move in faith, God will reveal the direction in which we should go, one step at a time. God will send us the help and strength we need. God is calling us to a higher level of God's glory. The choice is ours; let us answer the call and allow the faith that God has given us to be the catalyst for our success, our victory in Christ, and experiencing the miracles of God.

The Healing of Greg Harrison Through Prayers of Faith (in the words of Sarah Harrison)

The following is an account of God's healing grace that not only brought about physical healing, but the greatest healing of all—God's salvation through Jesus Christ:

"On August 28, 2002 at five thirty in the morning, I took my husband, Gregory Harrison, to Christiana Care Hospital in Newark, Delaware for a routine preventative heart catheterization procedure. Around eight, the cardiologist and other physicians were shocked to learn that the left anterior descending artery (often called the 'widow maker') was 80 percent blocked and required immediate open heart surgery. The surgery took place at ten and was considered a successful triple bypass surgery.

"Greg was moved from recovery to the Cardiac ICU early in the afternoon. He was receiving medication to coagulate his blood, but it was not working. As a pharmaceutical health professional and passionate health advocate, I became very concerned about the significant bleeding which continued despite the treatment. I mentioned my concern to the nurse, who consulted the surgeon and the other healthcare professionals. They decided to take him back to the operating room to open his heart again and address the bleeding.

"I contacted my former pastor since I hadn't met the new pastor. Both pastors, Rev. Harmon and Rev. Penn, came to the hospital while Gregory was in the operating room. They both prayed with me and only left the hospital after we learned that Gregory was stable and in recovery.

"Around eleven that night, I was allowed to see him. I felt that he was not out of danger because the blood was still flowing like a hose pipe through several rather large, clear tubes. They were giving him blood and using the best blood clotting agent available, fresh frozen plasma. It seemed to me that the blood transfusion was going in and flowing out simultaneously. I finally left the room, hoping the new more potent agent would work.

"I sent my sons Broderick and Brandon home; another son, Ahmad, stayed with me. I tried to rest, but after midnight I saw a frightening vision of Greg in distress. His face was dark red. Almost immediately, after seeing the vision, the attending physician came in and asked what medications Greg was on. Then he said they had to take him back to the operating room because he was going into multiple organ failure. His platelets were abnormally low, his blood pressure extremely low, and he was still bleeding. I remembered that his prescribed medications were in my purse. When I looked at them I became weak as I suddenly realized that two of them were blood thinners. I then asked for a new surgical team.

"After the attending physician left, I called Rev. Harmon and Rev. Penn to advise them of the need to take Greg back to the OR. I asked them to pray but not to come until I notified them. Within minutes the ICU nurse ran in and screamed, 'We are losing him, and we can't even move him to the operating room due to his deteriorating condition!'

"I raised my hands and called out the name of Jesus. I turned to see Rev. Penn standing there behind me, even though I suggested he not come. The surgeon had returned from her home and begged me to let her handle the dire situation. I asked Rev. Penn to pray over her so that she would decrease and God would work through her. Ahmad ran out to find out what was happening to his dad. I later learned they told him they thought Greg was clinically dead.

"It was now after two in the morning of August 29. I was very upset that Greg's health had become life threatening. His bleeding had not stopped, and the doctors had told me they had done all they could do. I called Rev. Penn at home and explained that Greg was in a life-or-death situation. I asked him to pray for Greg. 'He needs a miracle'; I blurted out, trying to keep from crying. Rev. Penn reminded me that where two or more would touch and agree on anything we ask the Father in Jesus' name, it would be done by the Father. He began to pray in the Spirit, using his prayer tongues because he did not know how to pray for Greg.

"After praying for about ten minutes, he paused and whispered a prayer, asking the Holy Spirit how he should pray for Greg's healing. Instantly he received the word that he should pray for Greg's salvation. Rev. Penn shared this with me and began to intercede for Greg's salvation. In his prayer, he asked the Holy Spirit to touch Greg's heart, mind, and will, giving him the assurance of God's love. He continued, asking the Holy Spirit to help Greg to ask God to forgive his sins and to save him. Then Rev. Penn began to call on the power of the blood of Christ. I interrupted him, saying, 'Yes, the blood of Jesus.' So we joined together, praying for the power of the blood of Jesus. Rev. Penn continued, praying, 'Lord Jesus, stop the bleeding in Greg's body.' He continued to call on the power of the blood of Christ Jesus. By this time Rev. Penn and I were agreeing that the blood would cleanse Greg of his sins and make him well and whole.

"After about half an hour, Rev. Penn closed the prayer for Greg with thanksgiving and praise to God. He thanked God for His healing power. He thanked God for hearing our prayers for Greg's salvation and his complete healing. Rev. Penn reminded me that salvation was the greatest healing of all. Salvation is ultimate healing.

"For a brief moment I was confused by his prayer concerning salvation. Then suddenly I had an out-of-body experience. I was thrust into the OR, and I could see a vision that appeared to be God himself come down from heaven and take over. He took Greg's heart in his hands and shaped and molded it; then he placed Greg's heart back in his body and filled Greg with new blood. I was then thrust back into my seat with a peace I had never felt in my life. I knew God's will had been done.

"By this time, Broderick, Brandon, and Rev. Harmon had returned. When Rev. Harmon asked me about Greg, all I could say was 'God's will has been done.' When I went back upstairs, Rev. Penn greeted me and told me the doctor had reported that Greg was stable. I wasn't sure how to react because they had reported that previously. I left Rev. Penn and went to the chapel to praise and thank God.

"Around six o'clock they allowed me to come to the ICU room. When I saw Greg, I knew he was fine despite the numerous tubes, machines, swelling, respirator, and everything else. There were only a few droplets of blood in the tubes, proof that the bleeding had stopped. The new shift of doctors and specialists, the head nurse, and others were reviewing charts and examining him. The head physician and the head nurse were discussing his current test results and body functions and could not believe his quick recovery. They said, 'This doesn't correlate to his previous vital signs. How can this be?' Everything was back to normal, and I was praising and thanking God for Greg's resurrection, his new life.

"Everyone involved, especially the surgeon, the ICU nurse and others who had been in the OR, admitted that it was a miracle. They just couldn't explain it. I knew it was a miracle, and I knew it was for me to see so I would know how powerful God really is.

"After several days, when Greg was able to talk, he shared with the family what had happened to him while he was in the operating room. While he was still in an unconscious state and the doctors had given up hope; somehow he felt a strong urge to ask God to forgive him of his sins. He asked Jesus to come into his heart. That was the moment Greg's health condition changed and he began to improve. Greg's account of his communication with God in the operating room confirmed how the Holy Spirit had led Rev. Penn to pray for him. Greg's health improved steadily hour by hour. We give God all of the praise and glory for Greg's miraculous healing.

"We called that day, August 29, 2002, Greg's new birth date. He was born again, and I think I was also born again. I will never forget that day. I truly think that Rev. John Penn prayed the prayer that was answered immediately by God the Father, Son, and Holy Spirit. I am eternally grateful for his obedience and powerful healing prayers.

"Thirteen years have passed, and Greg is doing well. We are blessed, but we are still challenged by many distractions, and we haven't faithfully answered God's calling on our lives. Please pray for us."

Author's Note: Scripture reveals that *"the prayer offered in faith will make the sick person well; the Lord will raise him up. If he has sinned, he will be forgiven. ...The prayer of a righteous man [or woman] is powerful and effective"* (James 5:15-16b). God is faithful.

Stepping Out in Faith to Trust the Lord

Stepping out in faith is sometimes what it takes for us to see God work in a mighty way. I am reminded of this by my husband, John's, healing miracle in 2013. In this miracle, God worked through the doctors, as well as independently of any man or woman. In April 2013, John awoke and called me to look at what looked like red dots covering his legs. There were also red-looking bruise marks on his back. I had never seen anything like it, so I suggested that John call the doctor and have him to take a look. John also had dental appointment that day, so he decided to call the doctor for an appointment, and while waiting for the doctor to return his call, go on to his dental appointment. During his appointment, John received a call from the doctor's office saying that he could come in. The time fell right into place, scheduled immediately after his visit to the dentist.

The internist drew some of John's blood and informed him that he would be notified later of the results. The next morning John received a call at 5:00 a.m. The doctor told John to go to the hospital immediately. His blood platelets were down to 2,000. We didn't know that a normal blood platelet count is 140,000 to 300,000.

The doctor he was to see at the hospital is an oncologist. Upon arrival, I was amazed to find out he was actually sent to the cancer center. Shortly after he arrived at the hospital for the appointment, he was quickly taken into a room where more blood was drawn by the nurse. A few minutes later he was told that his blood platelets were at 6,000 and he would be admitted to the hospital immediately for a protocol of steroids to correct the problem. The word *steroid* lit up my mind like a light bulb. I knew from my own reading that steroids can be helpful, but they can also have dangerous side effects. My daughter, Jacqueline had suffered a bad side effect from steroids. I questioned the doctor about the use of the steroid and asked if there were any alternatives. She said no. Even when I explained my concerns, she continued to insist that there were no alternatives. She was a young oncologist with a very nice bedside manner, but I still felt no peace about the treatment to be used.

I was dumbfounded. What do you do in a situation like this? I could only pray and allow the doctor to have her way. I didn't want to jeopardize the health of my loved one by making a decision that could be fatal. After all, I knew nothing about this health concern called ITP (idiopathic thrombocytopenic purpura) which involves blood platelet levels dropping to such an extremely low level and becoming life threatening. If not treated, it may lead to uncontrollable bleeding.

John was admitted to the hospital and told he would have to stay about two days. Within a few hours, John was started on the protocol. The IV of medication, including the steroids, was connected to John's arm; it took about twelve hours to complete. Shortly after that, another medication was given. It took me some time to realize that this follow-up medication was for the side effects.

At the end of a long day, I went home and immediately began to do hours of research concerning the medication, the health concern, and possible alternatives. My research confirmed my thinking, which I do not doubt was led by the wisdom of God.

By the second day of John's stay in the hospital, I had taken quite a few notes. I called a medical center in California that used alternatives to convention medicine, and I read about others who had this health concern. I learned that, indeed, the medication could have severe side effects. Through reading testimonies of those who did get well and continued to be well over a long period of time, I learned they had used alternative methods. I was quite impressed by one testimony that gave great details on the approach that helped him. He tried alternative treatments—vitamins, wheat grass, healthy foods, and a vegan diet— that built up his immune system. Those who relied only on the doctor's medication continued to return to the hospital quite often.

After taking the steroid medication twice, John began to complain that he didn't feel right in his chest area. He related this to the nurses, but they just stood at a distance and listened to him without responding. I became quite concerned, and as I left the hospital, I decided to call his doctor. The doctor I called was substituting for John's doctor. When I related my husband's concern, the doctor flew back question after question: "What do you mean he has discomfort in his chest?" "Why didn't the nurse tell me this?" Tell the nurse to call me." He finally backtracked and said, "I'll tell her myself."

When we hung up, I called John to let him know a nurse would be coming. Sure enough, the nurse entered the room while John and I were on the telephone. I could hear her say, "The doctor wants to know what kind of pain you are having." John replied, "I don't have any pain, but I just don't feel right."

Right then and there, I decided that if God would be my guide and help, I was getting John out of that hospital.

John had been told that if things went well and his platelets came up to 40,000, he could go home after two days. Despite John's discomfort, in two days his platelets did come up to 40,000. We were looking forward to him going home, but I had the distinct warning in my spirit, that they were going to want him to remain in the hospital for two more days. I told John, "I think they're going to ask you to stay two more days, even though your platelets are up to 40,000. So be ready and know what to say." John agreed.

Sure enough, on Saturday morning I was there to take John home when the doctor's nurse came in and spent forty-five minutes trying to convince him to stay two more days. John steadfastly insisted this was a step of faith to take the time to allow God to do God's work and not solely depend on medication. The only way they allowed him to go home was if he agreed to come back on the next Wednesday. We agreed.

I felt strongly led to make an appointment with a naturopathic doctor, who had a Ph.D in nutrition. I was able to make an appointment for the coming Monday. After interviewing John, she had his blood drawn and sent to a special laboratory to determine what his body was lacking and what was needed to build up a strong immune system. The lab report would take ten days to complete, but I was thankful that the Lord had made it possible to see this doctor so quickly. She gave us hope that there was a more natural approach to the healing of John of ITP.

On the following Wednesday, John returned to the hospital. Again, John's blood was tested to determine his blood platelet count. When the nurse returned, her first words were, "Your blood platelets are up to 300,000." Spontaneously, I said, "Praise God!" The nurse responded, "I guess the medicine did work." Without thinking, I said, "It's not the medicine; it's God." That stopped the nurse in her tracks, but as we left, she said, "It's a good thing you didn't stay those two days." After all my research, I knew without a doubt that if John's platelets went that high in just three days after leaving the hospital, it had to be more than medication. It had to be God.

John was required to come back to the hospital for two more Wednesdays. On one visit, the doctor gave the impression that she wasn't too happy when his platelets were now about 90,000. John came back with a worried and unhappy expression, but God gave me the wisdom to know that the count was just fine. I said, "Now your body is working on its own, and that is really good." My research had indicated that as long as the platelet count was 50,000, there was no reason to be alarmed.

Later, John was assigned to a doctor closer to where we live in Canton, Georgia. An elderly doctor, he was very encouraging and pleased with John's progress. After meeting with him for the next three weeks, this doctor told John he was doing fine and no longer needed to meet with him to check his progress. Meanwhile, as John waited on the report from the laboratory sent by the naturopathic doctor, he had gone on a completely vegan diet, eating salads, juicing from organic carrots, drinking wheat grass and aloe vera juice, and taking more vitamins. Finally, the report came back, containing several detailed pages of what vitamins to take and what John's body needed, as well as areas in which he was doing well. We had most of the supplements that John was recommended to take in our kitchen cabinet. So along with the vegan diet and juicing carrots, aloe vera juice, and wheatgrass, John intentionally took the supplements and we added those we did not have. Two years have passed since John was in the hospital, and he has been doing well with no recurrence of ITP or any of its symptoms.

When John had his last regular yearly physical, his platelet count was 170,000 and has remained in that range since his illness. God is truly good and does reward our faith. Even more, this is a testimony to God's faithfulness and love to those of us who are God's children. Sometimes, all we need to do is step out in faith with our complete trust in God, and God will more than meet us half way. God does work in mysterious marvelous ways, God's wonders to perform!

Appendix

Sermon: Love and Compassion Without Limitations

Jesus came to express and give evidence of the love of God, for the love of God is without limitations. One such account of God's healing love is when Jesus, after having a very busy day, decides to cross to the other side of a lake. He has just delivered a man who was possessed by a legion of demons. But, when he crosses the lake, he finds himself surrounded by a crowd of people. Suddenly, a man falls on his knees, begging him with tears to come and heal his dying daughter. This man is Jairus, a ruler of the synagogue. Now, Jairus is not just a "nobody;" in his time and in his community, he is an important "somebody," a person recognized by his peers as upstanding and a man of authority. Yet, this man of wealth and influence is at the feet of Jesus, begging Jesus for the life of his daughter. Jairus clearly recognizes the extraordinary power of Jesus to do miracles. He says, *"My little daughter is dying, please come and put your hands on her so that she will be healed and live"* (Mark 5:23). The Scripture says simply, *"so Jesus went with him"* (Mark 5:24). Jesus recognizes in Jairus a strong sense of belief and sincerity that he could heal his daughter. Besides this, we know that Jesus has a special love for children. So Jesus, without hesitation, proceeds to follow Jairus to his home. You see, *Jesus is a man of power; Jesus is a man of action; Jesus is a man of love and compassion.*

Now, as Jesus proceeds to the home of Jairus, the large crowd follows along with them. In this crowd is a woman who has been bleeding for twelve years. This woman not only suffers from her infirmity, but she suffers rejection by those in her community because, according to their Levitical laws, anyone who comes in contact with her is considered ceremonially unclean (Lev. 15:19-33). But this does not stop her. Even though she has been suffering for twelve years and has spent all of her money on doctors, somehow she still has hope that, with Jesus, she can be healed.

As she comes up behind Jesus and touches his cloak, her thoughts reveal her faith and determination to receive a miracle: *"If I may touch his garment, I shall be whole"* (Matt. 9:21 KJV). The Scripture reads that immediately, yes immediately, her bleeding stops and she has that feeling, throughout her body, that she is freed from her suffering (v. 29). The Word of God tells us that as a man thinks in his heart, so is he. This woman believes in her heart and so it is done. Still, it's not going to be quite that simple, because *Jesus discerns that something has happened; he discerns that power has gone out from him.*

We know that Jesus was and is full of the Holy Spirit. Jesus knows that power has gone out from him; he wants to know exactly what has happened, so he asks, *"Who touched my clothes?"* The disciples wonder why Jesus would be asking such a question when so many people are pressing against him in the crowd. Other people were pressing around Jesus, trying to touch him, but the difference is that *when this woman touches him, she touches him with purpose.* She

Sermon: Love and Compassion Without Limitations

wants to be healed, and she touches Jesus with the purpose of being healed. She wants a miracle. Jesus in turn knows this was not just an ordinary touch. You see, it wasn't just the fact that someone has touched him, but Jesus knows that someone has received something from him—not from his cloak, but from him. So, Jesus continues to look around until the woman comes forth and admits that she is the one who touched him.

You know sometimes, I am just perplexed as to why there are those that Jesus does so much for, yet they hesitate to come forth and tell what the Lord has done for them. Jesus does not let this woman get away with God's blessing without telling anyone. A great and wonderful miracle has been performed in her life. After twelve long years of suffering, she has been healed. After twelve long years, she has been made whole.

So, the woman comes forth and tells Jesus the truth. Jesus says to her, with love and compassion, *"Daughter, your faith has healed you. Go in peace and be freed from your suffering"* (v. 34). What is Jesus trying to do when he wants to know who touched him—embarrass the woman? No, Jesus is letting those who are present witness God's unlimited love and compassion. He is letting them know that this woman who has been rejected, who Satan has kept in suffering and pain for twelve long years; who is considered hopeless in the eyes of the world, has been freed by the greater power of God, in Christ.

There are those in our society today, perhaps even in the church, who, if others knew their illness, would be rejected. They are rejected and suffering in pain because of the world's way of thinking. They feel hopeless that no one can help them. But there is someone who cares, someone who will free us if we only reach out and touch him. And as we reach out, the devil will have to flee. The Word of God tells us to resist the devil and he will flee from us. As we draw near unto God, God will draw near unto us (James 4:7-8). Jesus came to demonstrate the unlimited love and compassion of our God. Jesus came to save us all and give us victory over the challenges of life. Just as this woman was restored to health and wholeness, and then restored to her community, Jesus came to restore us to life and community.

But this is not the end of the story. Even as Jesus is speaking to the woman, some men come from the house of Jairus to tell him his daughter is dead and he should not bother the teacher anymore. But Jesus ignores them and tells the synagogue ruler, *"Don't be afraid; just believe"* (Mark 5:36). You know, sometimes, we just have to ignore the negativity of others and keep going. We can't let the negative thoughts and words of others stop us from going forth and doing the will of God. Furthermore, if we are going to receive our miracle, we can't let the negativity of others keep us from moving in faith towards God's promises for our life and the lives of God's people. Although at times, it can be very difficult, we can't let others keep us from activating our faith and trust in an almighty, amazing, and awesome God. We have to ignore the naysayers and walk on with God.

Jesus not only ignored those with unbelief, but he allowed only Peter, James and John to go with him to see Jarius's daughter. He separated himself from the very presence of those who were in conflict with what he was called to do. And again, sometimes we must separate ourselves from those who would pull us away from the things of God. Sometimes, those people can be religious, but if their religion and their theology are in conflict with the Word of God and the faith that God calls us to, we must choose God and not man. Peter said it this way, *"We must obey God, rather than men"* (Acts 5:29).

Sermon: Love and Compassion Without Limitations

When Jesus finally arrives at the home of Jairus, there is a sight to behold. He finds an atmosphere of confusion and a great deal of commotion with people crying, wailing, and flutes being played. Jesus tells them, *"The child is not dead but asleep."* But, instead of believing, they laugh at him. Jesus then puts them out and takes the parents with him, along with the three disciples. Sometimes, to accomplish the works and miracles of God, we must take along with us only those people we know are truly committed and, even when we don't want to, we must leave behind those who do not take God's work seriously. It's important that in our service to God, we surround ourselves with those people who truly believe in the truth of God's Word and are willing to act on God's Word in faith.

Once the atmosphere was receptive to the presence and power of God, Jesus took the child by the hand and with two simple words, *"Talitha Koum!"* (v. 41), which means, little girl, get up, the child immediately stands up and walks around. In the power of God, Jesus models for us the love and compassion of God and demonstrates that when we reach out and touch him, he is here. When we cry out to him in faith and trust, as Jairus did, he is here. When we reach out to him with a real purpose and declaration, as the woman with the issue of blood, he is here.

Here in these accounts, we see the contrast in the socioeconomic levels of these two persons—Jairus and the woman with the issue of blood. God's love is no respecter of persons. Jesus is truly one who shows us that God is a person of love and compassion with no limitations.

Sin, death, and disease were conquered because of the love and compassion of God, in Christ. We know that God so loved the world that he gave his only begotten Son so that we may experience eternal life and have an eternal relationship with God. Because of God's gifts of love to us through

Christ, we now have that same power to love and that same power to demonstrate the works of God. As people of God, we should also be people of love and compassion. Jesus did not simply request that we love one another; he commanded that we love one another and went on to say that others will know we are Christians by our love (John 13:34). When we do not accept this love, we allow ourselves to be unprotected and exposed to those spiritual forces that may cause damage to our *spirits, our minds, our bodies, and our relationships*. We have a choice, to act by faith in God's love and power, or to leave ourselves unprotected and exposed. God will fix it—the God of power, the God of mercy, and the God of love.

One essential truth that we must realize is God's power works through love and compassion. Haven't you read in Scripture that "faith works through love"? Therefore, in order to reveal God's power and healing grace to others, we too must have the love and compassion of God. Christ lives within those who have welcomed God into their hearts and lives. Those in whom Christ lives, have the power of the Spirit to love and have compassion. Through Christ and his authority we have the power of the Holy Spirit to do the miraculous works of God. Furthermore, Hebrews 2:4 indicates that God testifies to our salvation *"by signs, wonders and various miracles, and gifts of the Holy Spirit distributed according to his will."*

A most important purpose of Jesus and the miracles he performs in our lives is to bring us to a knowledge of his salvation and motivate us toward a closer relationship with God. When we lived in Newark, Delaware, I received a telephone call from a friend of mine. She was frantic and in tears; she had just found out that her husband had been previously married, not once but four times. Hers was his fifth marriage.

Sermon: Love and Compassion Without Limitations

I had no idea how I should respond to this news; I was at a loss for words. But it was as if the Lord had prepared me for this call. I had recently read the Scripture passage of 2 Corinthians 4:4, which reads, *"The god of this age has blinded the minds of unbelievers so that they cannot see the light of the gospel of the glory of Christ, who is the image of God."* As soon the Holy Spirit brought this verse to my mind, I knew that I was not to put her husband down or tell her that she should leave him, but I was supposed to pray that Scripture for his salvation. I said to her, "Let's pray." I then prayed that God would remove the scales from her husband's spiritual eyes so that he would be able to understand the love of God and receive salvation through Jesus Christ. I never dreamed that in the days to come, God would answer that prayer in such a unique way.

My friend invited John and me to her home to pray with her. We comforted and prayed with her for God's peace in her life and peace in her marriage. After the prayer, John prophesied that in seven days her husband would be saved. This was unusual for John; it even surprised him.

Shortly after this prayer request was made, John and I were invited to a neighbor's home for a get-together with other neighbors. Our neighbor, Mrs. Small, lived up the street from our house in an adjacent development. While we were fellowshipping with our neighbor and meeting her friends, we were surprised to see my friend, whom we had prayed with earlier, arrive with her husband.

We were about to leave to go home when my friend asked prayer for her back. Often a person will have back pains because one leg is shorter than the other. So, when my friend sat down for prayer, John measured her limbs. Sure enough, one limb was about an inch shorter than the other. At the time, she wore knee high boots with at least two inch heels. As John held her feet in his hands, I prayed with him that the shorter limb be lengthened to be even with the other leg. Almost before the prayer could be completed, her leg shot out.

My friend's husband witnessed this miraculous occurrence and became very emotional. Right then and there, John led him to salvation in Jesus Christ. He received the greatest miracle and healing of all—salvation. This occurred in seven days, as the Holy Spirit revealed. Some months later, they moved to Texas, and the last I heard, they were serving the Lord. God had again demonstrated God's miraculous power and mercy to heal both physically and spiritually. Through this simple but powerful miracle, the Holy Spirit made real, to my friend's husband the presence, the love, and compassion of the Living God. Now he has been forgiven of his sins, now he has been delivered from darkness into the marvelous light of God, and now he is no longer the same. Yes, God's love and compassion are without limitations.

Bibliography

Barclay, William. *The Gospel of John*, vol. 2, Philadelphia: The Westminster Press, 1975.

Clinebell, Howard. *Well Being*. Quezon City, Phillippines: Kadena Books, Claretian Publications, 1994.

Cone, James H. *Martin & Malcom & America*. Maryknoll, New York: Orbis Books, 1999.

Kelsey, Morton T. *Psychology, Medicine & Christian Healing*. San Francisco: Harper & Row Publishers, 1988.

Maddox, Randy L. *Responsible Grace*. Nashville, Tenn.: Kingswood Books, 1994

Wall, Robert W. *The Acts of the Apostles*, vol. X of The New Interpreter's Bible. Nashville, Tenn: Abingdon, Press 2002

Whitaker, Julian, M.D. *Reversing Heart Disease*. New York, NY: Warner Books, 2002

Worthington, Everett L. Jr. *Hope-Focused Marriage Counseling*. Downers Grove, Illinois:InterVarsity Press, 1999.

PERIORDICAL

_____"A Conversation with John Penn," *Alive Now,* Volume 31, No. 2. Nashville, TN: The Upper Room, 2001.

CPSIA information can be obtained
at www.ICGtesting.com
Printed in the USA
FFOW05n2022041215

9 781498 455169